And Mother Came Too

Joy Viney

SUMMERSDALE

Summersdale Publishers
46 West Street
Chichester
West Sussex
PO19 1RP

A CIP catalogue record for this book
is available from the British Library.

ISBN 1 873475 35 7

Printed in Great Britain.

Illustrated by
Sue Millar Smith

The names of some of the characters in this book
have been changed in order to protect their privacy.

Contents

Chapter 1..4
Chapter 2..13
Chapter 3..25
Chapter 4..33
Chapter 5..45
Chapter 6..56
Chapter 7..65
Chapter 8..77
Chapter 9..82
Chapter 10..94
Chapter 11..104
Chapter 12..114
Chapter 13..129
Chapter 14..145

CHAPTER 1

I was in the waiting lounge at Heathrow Airport, some flights had just been called and a young man and I were almost the only passengers left. He approached me.

"Excuse me, are you Freya Stark?"

Although very flattered I expostulated, "Surely, she must be years older than I?"

"Oh! , yes," he agreed, putting my mind at ease, "I meant when she was younger."

Vaguely puzzled and confused about the time factor, I was nevertheless thrilled for I had been mistaken for a great traveller when it was my first trip into the unknown and I was alone. Now I could hold my head a little bit higher.

I was a great admirer of Freya Stark and of all the earlier travelling ladies. Did I look a little bit like her I wondered? I didn't think so and I wasn't wearing anything like her famous hats. I am, I hope, sensibly dressed and have only one hat, a plain respectable sun hat to which, so far, no-one has taken exception. I do have several of the 'I wouldn't-be-seen-dead-with-you-in-that' sort but left these behind in case they gave the lions ideas.

I cannot hope to emulate Freya Stark's beautiful style or in any way follow in her eminent footsteps. For one thing I like to know where I'm going to lay my head at night. I am no longer young and have little faith in myself.

Neither can I pretend to follow in the footsteps of the other great lady travellers, especially those of the Victorian era with their great weight of clothing. These intrepid ladies such as Mary Kingstey or Isabella Bird Bishop travelled into the unknown with great courage, or was it ignorance? Did they, too, I wondered, as they faced the Dark Continent, have these butterflies in their insides?

Now I was here at Heathrow with my heart pounding but with a feeling of more confidence now that I had been mistaken for a celebrity and a real traveller, I must look the part even with my own knowledge of myself that, sadly, I was not a very exciting person and had never journeyed alone before. I had no desire to bike across Peru or climb in the Himalayas, all I wanted was a quiet trip, with a Safari or two, and Africa would do nicely for a start.

I told myself I preferred my anonymity, a celebrity's life must be very trying. I should hate the endless glances and followers that must be the fate of a television personality. It must be good publicity, it must also be very trying.

A sequence of events led me here to this doorway to the world. It all started in the hairdressers. I needed an experience of jolting realization to change my lifestyle. I was sitting in the hairdressers, the same one I had frequented for many years, and being ignored. I was, after all, only that old teacher from down the road who came in regularly on the same day every week for the same old hairstyle. I was no longer of any account as I could be relied upon to come again as it was near to the school and I could just get myself 'done' in the dinner hour. One of the assistants really knew about hair, sadly she left to join the police force, no doubt the force benefited but I continued to go there from habit.

On this particular day a jolly over curly girl called Shirley came bouncing up and suggested a 'little cover-up' for some of my increasing grey hairs.

"A bit of colour would look nice," she suggested in a honey coloured voice giving the impression of riotous ideas but eventually, disappointedly agreed that my own choice of a good mousey brown was more in keeping with the colour endowed by nature and more appropriate to my mode of life.

It was at this point that an unexpected rush order arrived. There was to be a party and three youngsters wanted something exciting done to their various heads and above all - NOW. The girls rallied round and this included Shirley. Alas! Forgotten was the mousey teacher, a regular who, of course, would come again next week! But would she? While viewing the overdark, overdry mess, the result of being 'overdone', something happened inside me and the old worm turned at last.

It was a grizzly grey sort of day too, and this added to my depression.

"This is what you have become," I told myself as I stepped out into a dismal world, "Not, as you had hoped to become, the sort of person who wandered nonchalantly into the travel agent and to have all the personnel there rise from their desks with looks of admiration and welcoming smiles."

Oh! Where had my dreams gone?

I had a feeling that it was now or never but how was I to achieve this?

Firstly, I decided, I would never return to that particular hairdresser and next was to turn my back on routine and take the first preliminary venture - into a travel agent. Then would turn my back on routine, gather together my resources and save for all I was worth.

"Admit that you are trapped in a rut," I said firmly to myself, "Give up the easy job, find something else."

Yes, it was a bit drastic. Why not a couple of weeks in Spain with everybody else during the school Summer holidays or Easter when it won't be quite so busy? I told myself it wasn't enough that I had become self satisfied with nothing.

It was chance that I cast an idle glance over the stars in that week's local paper. I read for Capricorn, "Sit back thinking the world owes you a living and you'll get nowhere fast. Get hyped up, motivate yourself and draw up a master plan for your conquest of the world. It sounds extreme but if you have a dream, aim or ambition you must pull out all the stops and develop an assertive, aggressive, winner-takes-all attitude!"

This certainly fitted in with my present mood and must have been written for me and so, not forgetting a quiet 'thank you' to Russell Grant, I resolutely advanced upon the travel agent.

I only knew one travel agent, Peter, and I didn't know him very well. I had met and talked with him in the local and once he had offered my son, Simon, a job which he refused. I now decided on a visit to his inviting premises and this is how I met Pearl and Chris. Peter acknowledged my presence but was far too engrossed in a hand injury he'd made with an electric carving knife, it was, indeed, a nasty mess. It needed redressing but no-one was volunteering to do it for him.

Pearl and Chris were giving lots of sympathy but wounds and bandaging were, quite definitely, not in their contracts. As a biology teacher such things have no horrors for me and I was willing to give them all this small service and received their gratitude. It was a good start as coffee was duly served. I was very nearly there!

It occurred to Pearl, grateful for my intervention, that I might be there for a purpose. Then came the obvious question.

"Is this a social visit?" she asked, with an eye to business.

"I am going to Africa," I said.

I was committed. All I had to do now was to reorganize my life.

Perhaps this sounds more drastic than it really was, I intended, as my first step into the unknown, to visit an old college friend. This friend, Paula, was now a widow and lived in Nairobi. My new ideas of myself visualized this courageous lone traveller following those great explorers to unknown parts of the globe, entirely self-sufficient, of course, carrying all I needed, walking, riding (a camel perhaps) and always looking into lofty mountains with lofty thoughts. How different reality, it was all a great fiction. I needed company, a fairly comfortable bed, preferably one to myself, certainly not in a crowded dormitory. I also like what are generally listed as 'facilities'. I often wonder how the Victorian ladies managed as I find so little mention of it in their writings.

My friend Paula has been inviting me to stay for years, so many times now that it had probably never occurred to her that I might accept. I hoped my, "Yes, thank you," would not cause a heart attack, and that it was a standing invitation and not just a habit. Her last letter had asked, "When are you coming?" and even more inviting, "I will save a trip to the coast until you come."

At this point I must justify my title. Yes, I am a Mother and I also have a husband, Tom. My daughter is called Amanda and my son Simon. Now Simon had wanted to travel ever since I read or invented bedtime stories. As a teacher I hoped to introduce and encourage an interest in Geography, even at his toddler stage.

(Amanda later went on to a good first degree in this subject so my time wasn't wasted) We travelled in imagination down many great rivers such as the Amazon and the Zambesi, magical names, Simon always finished and sleepily snuggled down, "And you must come, too."

Simon was now out there somewhere in an 'unsuitable-for-you, Mother' no-go area. (I think it was Angola) and I had only just started my own personal rebellion.

Tom? Well Tom is another story. Tom doesn't like holidays, he likes the security of his own things around him. He doesn't like lying on beaches, foreigners, animals and hasn't much tolerance for children. If he takes a holiday he takes it in January. Not in order to sun himself in the Antipodes, but so that no-one will worry him into, or expect him to take, a normal British Summer Holiday!

In Paula's last letter she wrote, "Tom would be very welcome but if he won't come then come without him." Could I? Remember this was before 'Shirley Valentine'.

It was settled for me by my doctor. Dr Campbell is an old fashioned doctor and a Scot of few words. I had gone to him with some very painful spots about my middle. He looked at me over the top of his glasses, "Shingles," he pronounced. "When did you last have a holiday?"

"I'm going out to Kenya for a long holiday." I said it firmly now and with conviction.

"Good," he said, "About time."

I went home and wrote to Paula. I thought about our friendship that had lasted so long and for the last twenty years on paper.

It was easy to get on with Paula. We had adjoining rooms in the students' hostel and a group of us often met over late night coffees. Although on different courses we had much in common, Paula was studying archaeology and I was set on a teaching career. I started going to evening art classes with her, art wasn't included in her syllabus and she said she needed it for drawing all the odd bits and pieces she hoped, one day, to find on a dig. She started coming home with me on shorter holidays when she was too broke to fly home, my family liked her too. At the end of our first year we decided to share a flat, it was badly furnished. gloomy and inconvenient but we were our own masters and it was cheap. It didn't look too bad, in fact it became quite cheerful when we had our own things about, especially African bits of Paula's. She had been born in Kenya and hoped to return there when she had finished her course. She spoke Swahili, which sounded very exotic to those of us offering the usual school French.

Things didn't turn out quite the way she expected for while I was looking down the Situations Vacant column for 'Teachers wanted for the Lower Fourth' she landed an excellent museum job with a Dr Greenway. Sam, Paula told me later, was a most interesting man, enthusiastic about his subject and it was some time before they discovered that they were also enthusiastic about each other. They may never have got round to it at all if they hadn't been working on the sexual habits of some ancient tribe, it was a natural sequence of events that they arrived at more recent cultural customs and practical work is always interesting.

They made their home in Nairobi in a suburb called Langata, near enough to the Wild Life Park to hear the roar of lions. Their enthusiasm for their archaeological work never seemed to wane.

Meanwhile I had married 'Maths-in-the-Upper School' and moved with him to the South Coast where he had taken over maths in the local Technical College. When two people have careers one has to give way on location, this, of course, had been me, not so difficult a decision at the time as a baby was on the way, Amanda was born and three years later Simon made his appearance. When they started school I took various teaching posts, not all of them satisfactory or suited to my particular talents. When this narrative started I had been for ten years at a large private school for girls and was considered a fixture.

Out in Kenya Sam and his driver were in a car crash. Sam died immediately, his driver lived long enough to keep muttering about a monkey, nobody ever knew quite what had happened. Paula was shattered and, except for a brief communication telling me of his death, I heard nothing for some time. Being Paula she came to terms with her widowhood and was determined to continue with the work they both loved. She wrote well and published several small books about the country. I had an early reply to my self invitation.

"You can't think how glad I shall be to see you again. I'm arranging some good trips, what fun it will be."

It was the old Paula. I was greatly cheered.

Breaking the news to Tom was another milestone. Is there any answer to, "What for?" when you are contemplating a new lifestyle? Its disheartening, especially when followed by, "What's the object of the exercise?" and, "Why go to an unknown place to stay with a friend you haven't seen in years?" I began to doubt my own decisions.

Don't get me wrong about Tom, he's fine so long as he is let alone, talk about engines and he becomes quite animated but he forgets things like birthdays and flowers and even Christmas, whether accidentally or on purpose I have yet to make up my mind. It certainly comes cheaper that way. I now decided it was no longer a joke and took a vow never to spend Christmas with him alone again. If he didn't want it he need not have it.

I carried on with my preparations and didn't answer the unanswerable questions. Amanda, when I told her said, "Well, why not?"

Simon was more definite, I rang him.

"Good for you," he said, "And next time, who knows...?"

I never knew what, it was a bad line and we were cut off.

Now all that remained, except the shopping, was to hand in my resignation at the school. This needed as much courage as telling Tom.

Our head would have made a good Minister of Education, and everyone knows where that can lead. She dismissed me in a way that meant she had better things to do than deal with mentally unstable women. I think the rest of the staff shared her views, voices ceased as I entered the Staff Room, was it imagination that I caught the phrase 'time of life'?.

"Anyone would think," I wrote to Paula, "that I was contemplating a life in the backwoods instead of a civilized holiday with an old friend in a definitely visitable country."

One friend, Joan, backed me and I was glad of her support.

"I've other ideas too," she said mysteriously. She would, I knew, tell me in her own good time.

I left a copy of one of Freya Stark's books in the staffroom hoping others might widen their views and get ideas. Education is, after all, a very good thing.

I left at the end of the summer term. As I was not departing until November I found a temporary job with the Milk Marketing Board.

The 'girls' I met were 'Bluebell' and 'Daisy', these days known as 29 or 36. It was a change. I could have gone on supply teaching but I preferred to have a complete break and think about teaching again on my return.

I'd become a bit of a miser and this without giving the question any consideration. My bank balance was healthier than I had expected, it happened because my Aunt Bea had died and left me a small legacy. Aunt Bea had been a great washer of small hands and faces and many times, preferring mine dirty, had I stuck my tongue out at her retreating back. Now, in retrospect, I withdrew it, sent her up a small prayer of thanks, and got down to the business of spending this unexpected windfall. Somehow I had added to this legacy, when I hadn't anything I hadn't bothered to save but a nucleus was enough to start off my miserly tendencies. Fortunately quickly subdued when I found I had enough for my fare and a bit of a splash on the shopping.

Amanda's son, my grandson George, came to stay, at the great age of eight he already had a mind of his own and was very fussy about my appearance as well as his own. I bought things on his advice and his positive attitude of, "Well-you-can't-go-wrong," which I now know could go very wrong indeed. Safari suits are for American tourists though the pockets are useful. The luggage was another case in point. It looked so good, all matching and including that 'absolute essential' organizer bag. It still looks good for I abandoned it long ago as I did some things labelled 'a-must-for-Safaris' which I left behind in Kenya. The luggage I offered to George last year as he had started on his travels and it was only sitting in a cupboard stuffed with 'it-might-come-in-useful-better-not-throw-it-away' rubbish. George declined it saying, "My old knapsack will do very nicely, thank you, but I wouldn't mind a new shirt." You can't win. He got his shirt, checks were in again and it was a check one he had added to his wardrobe on that shopping expedition instead of the purple roses he himself fancied, which I felt that his Mother would blame on me. Except for size these two check one were not dissimilar.

Back home we laid everything out and enthused over it, it was a different story later when I came to pack it for, even with the fancy cases bursting at the seams, there was still enough to stock a small boutique lying about the room.

This shopping expedition, especially seeing all that luggage, set me off dreaming again, I saw myself with my bearers carrying all my clutter on their heads, there was a fine picture in one of the travel books to which I had become addicted. It showed a long column of men with the 'fever-weakened' traveller also being carried in a sort of hammock. Fever? I came to earth with a bump and jerked myself back to today for, not only would I have to carry my own luggage, no-one would be likely to carry me. Most important of all, what did I do about fever? There are certain advantages for today's travellers, there are modern medicines. What did I need in the way of injections and was there still danger from malaria? So it was back to Dr Campbell again. He had all the answers, malaria is best prevented, not only by taking tablets but by using insect repellents and covering up at night. He didn't think it necessary to carry a mosquito net, a pity, I rather fancied this unusual addition to my baggage. Yellow fever immunization can only be obtained from special clinics, there was one in Bournemouth. The waiting room housed a motley collection of interesting travelling characters, I could have stayed chatting all morning but my name was called, I was scratched, received my certificate and was all set for the fever ridden jungle of my imagination.

So I was ready at last, my taxi arrived and Tom waved me off in a very bewildered way, he had never believed that I would go and was considerably worried about the cooking as, for him, scrambled egg is a risky venture into the culinary arts.

At the last minute I nearly changed my mind but I remembered those intrepid Victorian lady travellers as well as that early forgotten forecast from my stars. Where was my free spirit? I thought I'd freed it even if my heart was in my mouth. It gave me strength to think of all those other lovely courageous, indomitable Capricorns.

I have reached the airport, I have booked in, my luggage has gone and I am having coffee with the young man who thinks I look like Freya Stark, and my adventures are about to begin.

CHAPTER 2

It was a night flight and I saw nothing of the vast desert that I had seen so often in my school atlas, wondered about and longed to see the reality.

At dawn we came down to refuel at Khartoum and I saw my first glimpse of real poverty. Women were scavenging on large rubbish heaps and I thought that leftover scraps from our plastic dinners would probably keep several families for a week.

We arrived a Nairobi airport on a lovely morning at about breakfast time. I am fairly used to African airports by now but my first arrival induced a terrible panic. These days it would be called culture shock. There were forms to fill in and I couldn't find my glasses, it dawned on me that I had no address to go to only a box number. I had a brand new passport, later it became a document of excitement and variety but this first time it seemed all I had to cling to, something that told me "Yes," this was me but with no idea of what I was doing there.

In the thrusting crowd I saw an approachable face. Anxiously I asked, "I have no address to go to only a box number, what do I do?"

"Put that down," he said "No-one's going to read it."

Later someone told me to put down the most expensive hotel if in any doubt as this looks good.

I believe it is a good thing to have 'teacher' on one's passport. Mine is genuine but I have heard that people in doubt as to their status also put it down - this looks like cheating.

Now the official looked at it, looked at me, "Teacher?" "Yes," a smile and I was through. Since those days I have had "What do you teach?" "Do you still teach?" and even "Is it good to teach in England?" Then I feel we could hold up the queue for hours with a meaningful discussion.

My panic passed, or nearly so for it was at this point that I realised I hadn't seen my friend for more than twenty years. Should I know her again?

I thought a helpful porter would be money well spent, one hurried up to me with a trolley and managed to convey to me that he would be very willing to accept some currency other than African shillings, say dollars or pounds. He swept me through customs and there was Paula waving madly.

"I was so worried," she said "I was afraid I might not recognise you, but you look exactly the same and so English!"

I am English, how was I supposed to look.

It was the same old Paula, the years slipped away and for a moment it seemed that we were two students again.

I think I fell in love with Africa as I merged into the morning sun, so bright, warm and cheerful after the gloom of an English November day. The contrast was heady. Why was this called the Dark Continent I wondered, even the soil was a rich red and the trees and flowers were brilliant. I should have to get used to the idea that I didn't know any names and promised myself that on the first shopping expedition I should buy some books on flowers, shrubs and possibly birds of Kenya. It turned out that Paula had most of these but I didn't know that at the time.

Paula lived in a suburb called Langata. There was plenty of ground rather heavily fenced in which I soon learned was essential, it looked strange to me coming from very open English countryside.

The bungalow was long and low, it looked roomy and comfortable, there was a wide veranda running the whole length of the building. Creeper with bright orange flowers was climbing up one end, there was a Bougainvillaea on the other side, this I did recognize but other trees and shrubs had me mystified.

"Isn't that a banana tree?" I asked Paula.

"Yes," she replied, "But the monkeys take most of them."

Now I knew I wasn't in Dorset.

The ground sloped down to some small buildings, Paula pointed them out as the servants' quarters. I supposed I would have to get used to servants and, as a man came quickly out to get my luggage, I thought it was something that I could accustom myself to very easily.

I have my own faithful Mrs Mop who comes in one morning a week and I think myself lucky to get her but this could hardly be compared to Paula's two men and a girl. I probably paid my good lady helper as much as one of these.

"I've put you in the guest house," said Paula, "It has everything there and this door opens onto the veranda."

Yes, it had everything, it was almost too good to be true but I felt feelings of guilt, I was, after all, supposed to be living rough and hard as had some of my heroines. After unpacking I tried out the bed as it looked so comfortable, not at all the coarse camp bed I should be enduring, nor did the man, Kimani, look like someone willing to carry me over a swamp. I had no intention of sleeping and was surprised when I heard a voice calling to come and have a drink before supper. It seemed to be growing dark, my timing was out, this must be jet lag.

I had slept deeply, this was no hard bed and the nearest I'd come to a bearer was the trolley porter at the airport.

I joined Paula on the veranda.

"How long are you staying?" she asked.

"Three months," I replied. She stared at me open mouthed while I rushed for my duty free bottle. After the first drink she said, "I could take a bit of a holiday and a few days off here and there ..." After the second she said, "If you'd stayed with me every year for a week that would have been twenty weeks, this will only be twelve!"

Paula was always good at statistics. We were silent for a while with our thoughts and our drinks. It was during the third and after a good pause for thinking that I said, "I don't have to stay here all the time."

"But I'd like you to," she said. This was a good beginning. We had some mutual friends, an ex-policeman who had been on the air to Tom in his Radio Ham days. He and his wife Dorothy had invited me to stay, they knew Paula slightly. I thought I would accept and give Paula a break from me.

"I could also hire a vehicle or go on a truck," I said "Or a camel," I added gaining confidence, thinking of my twenty porters and letting the dream fade.

"It all sounds a good idea," said Paula, "And what you don't do this time you can do next time."

I looked at the bottle and its decreasing contents and hastily returned it to the cupboard in case I got to living there permanently.

I had a few quiet days whilst Paula got ahead with her office work, I made an effort to get to know the garden wildlife and the neighbours. On one side a delightful Kenyan mother told me that I could use the children's swing at any time. I found this rather endearing and I couldn't imagine anyone back home even suggesting that I should enjoy it.

Wandering further afield and behind some trees I saw a small wooden colonial looking building. A white woman emerged with a cigarette dangling from her mouth and a very displeased expression. She grumbled something at me, Kimani was right behind me and made chopping movements with his machete.

"No, no," I said and he laughed uproariously. No doubt it was a joke, I hoped it was and preferred to think so. I began to like Africans as well as Africa.

"She's been there for years," said Paula when I told her of my encounter with her neighbour, "She may drop in to coffee one day when she is in the mood, or when she runs out of her own. She's a Kenyan citizen, an old Post Office worker I think."

During these early days I realized that Paula, too, needed a break. She'd been working hard on publicity pamphlets as well as her own writing, together we started planning our various outings.

Our very first trip was into Nairobi Game Park. This could hardly be called a safari although while we were eating our picnic lunch in one of the lookouts I was able to have some idea of the vastness of the plains.

This park has a Langata gate so was not far away. I had no idea that there was a park of this size so near to the town. Paula said she had heard lions roaring in the night. We drove around all day and it seemed wonderfully remote in spite of being able to see the Nairobi skyline in the distance. We saw great herds of buffalo as well as giraffe, gazelle, ostrich and even a rhino. The most exciting was a cheetah after a kill but my favourite was a family of warthogs with two delightful babies trotting behind. The birds were wonderful but even with Paula to identify them I didn't seem to be able to take in all the names.

Before I write any more of our jaunts I must point out that I am not writing a guide book nor am I giving lists of African animals. Lists of animals are pretty meaningless. There are many informative travel books written by people with far more knowledge of the country than I. This is my own personal story, the story of my desire for travel and my own way of going about it. It's about my own reactions to this wonderful country, its people, its atmosphere and its own unique smell, that warm smell you never forget.

There are books too, with wonderful photographs of animals and I'm no photographer. I do have a few, a distant long neck, a grey fat lump in a muddy pool, the back end of a departing elephant and some rather doubtful stripes disappearing into the background, a wonderful example of camouflage I tell myself. I have some good bird nests too, but if there were any birds they sensibly flew off at the sight of my clumsy approach.

One day Paula said, "Pack a small bag, I have a pilot friend who has offered us a seat up to Keekorok, it's a wonderful place, put in a swimsuit - there's a pool there! Do you want to come?"

Did I?

Paula seemed to have knocked up a lot of brownie points in the way of favours. "Some other time," she would have said and now the time had come, she'd needed a companion, I was lucky to come at just the right time. Up to now I had felt guilty at having planted myself on her but now it seemed that the benefits were mutual. We set out to enjoy ourselves. "It's a lodge in the Masai Mara and we leave from Wilson Airport," said Paula.

This was a small airport, not the large Jomo Kenyatta International Airport where I'd arrived, the plane we were to travel in was as small and neat as the girl who was to fly it. It was an interesting flight as this pilot seemed more fascinated by my shirt than in her task. I promised to send her one like it hoping it would help her to concentrate. I wasn't sure, by the way she kept peering down, if she knew the way but maybe I was mistaken when I thought I heard her say that Daddy had let her take it up.

Under us were all the small African farms or shambas, each growing a wide variety of produce for their own needs. It was green and fertile.

We landed safety at Keekorok Lodge, we were greeted warmly and shown to our chalet. These were delightful stone cottages with cedar shingle roofs and all facilities. The lunch was excellent, there was a atmosphere of excitement in the air for a staff football match was planned, a rival team arrived and everyone trooped out to watch.

I hadn't come to Kenya to watch football matches but I joined the crowd, it seemed a happy event.

I wasn't at all sure what was happening on the field, it didn't seem to have much in common with the matches that are on television so endlessly in Britain. Curiously enough I found no desire to switch it off. There were some unconventional features and a great many personal feuds. During one argument a player sat on the ball and refused to give it up and as the referee seemed as uncertain of the rules as everyone else the game only resumed when the hotel manager arrived and shouted at everyone, this included the man on the ball who allowed it into the game once more.

The audience had drifted away as it was getting dark, I seemed to be about the last spectator except Paula with her camera at the ready. The cup arrived and as no-one was there to present it it was handed to me. I was surprised that any final score had been arrived at but was perfectly willing to oblige. I shook hands all round, perhaps they thought I was someone. I got a bit above myself and offered to 'put on the hands' when I saw someone was injured. He accepted, I did and he said it was better. Perhaps I have the gift!

It was dark and too late for watching four-legged animals and for swimming. We showered, dressed in our best (newly acquired long African robes) and went into the main building for dinner. This was excellent as was the after-dinner entertainment. This was a spectacular Masai dance, the warriors dressed in red with red ochre hair, beads and spears jumped from on-the-spot to a surprising height. After watching for some time I began to recognize some of the footballers now in a very different dress. What a wonderful way to develop the kicking muscles.

One writer, Jan Hemsing, describes Keekorok as a very happy place. I think I agree with her.

In the middle of the night, or at the crack of dawn depending on your viewpoint, I felt someone shake me.

"Joy, are you awake?" said Paula.

"I am now," I replied sleepily, hoping she would go away.

"There's a space on a balloon trip, do you want to go?"

I WAS awake.

"Give me five minutes, go and tell them I'm coming."

After all who is going to bother if I wash or not in a balloon. I was out in three minutes, hat and jacket in hand in case it was sunny or cold or both, telling myself delightedly that none of the Victorian lady travellers had ever ventured up in a balloon.

"You won't have to pay, the pilot's a friend of mine, he offered it to me but I may get another chance - you won't," shouted Paula at my retreating back. I was in time to see the balloon filled and then the pilot and passengers climbed into the basket.

I have a certificate for this flight. It says I showed courage but there is no mention of my amusement at the other passengers. While I had no luggage the Americans were hung about with vast amounts of ironmongery. I had even forgotten my camera and I think if I had all those gadgets I should have missed the wonder of all the animals below. We swept silently through the air with only an occasional reheating of the air and viewed all around us the seemingly endless expanse of Africa.

My certificate also gives the list of animals we saw, I don't think I recognized all of them at the time and especially from up above, but I do remember my amazement at the huge numbers and my pleasure at seeing elephants with babies.

We landed for a champagne breakfast, the balloon was packed away and we drove back to the lodge, seeing more animals, this time at their own level.

We had time for a swim before the plane left again, one of these days I must go back.

Paula had to educate me on archaeological matters, she wanted to revisit Olorgesaile, an important prehistoric site full of early hand axes which had been beside a now dried-up lake. The sort of place where you can imagine man really did originate. I was not entirely ignorant and wanted to see the place. We started my education at the Nairobi Museum where various objects were now housed. This put me in the picture and helped to work up my enthusiasm.

"There are self-help bandas there," Paula said. "Huts to you, we can camp in these, see if you can find the old camping gear, there should be sleeping bags and things." I looked and certainly found 'things'. Sorting this out and cleaning it took some time, I don't think it had been used since Sam died.

"It'll be hot," said Paula.

It was. This was the hottest I'd been.

It was an exciting place. There was a small museum and a sensible guide. It was not overcrowded. Later another party arrived and in the evening we all sat round a camp fire which we built 'to keep the lions away' as someone suggested. We were able to cook up some soup and we shared our various tins. I, for one, didn't sleep much, imagining lions in every sound and there were plenty in the warm African night. But I did feel it was the real thing at last.

Years ago as a school girl in a Geography lesson I had promised myself a visit to the great Rift Valley. It was a warm day, the windows were open and so was my atlas, Africa lay before me. "One day," I was telling myself, "I shall go there." It was a wonderful day for dreaming which ended when I was brought up sharply by a question I hadn't heard. Geography was different in those days, you were expected to know maps and locate the coal fields.

The Rift Valley is an amazing region stretching from the Red Sea right down into Zambia, there are many lakes in the valley, some deep, some shallow, some are fresh water, some soda lakes. There are wonderful escarpments and every Geologist wants to go there, or the sight of it makes you want to become one.

We did day trips to most of the lakes, Nakura is a soda lake with a vast population of flamingos, they form a pink haze. I think I might have become confused if we had had one long trip, taking a day or two days with our camping equipment I was able to enjoy the valley and its wildlife especially these lake birds. There were pelicans as well as flamingos and we also saw vultures. I discovered I was not too fond of these scavengers, I know they do an excellent job of cleaning up but I do not want to know the details.

So we visited this string of lakes, Navarsha which is fresh, Magadi and Begoria which are soda. We stayed a while in Baringo where hippos came very near our camp. Begoria has hot springs, it was quite frightening to see the mud bubbling and to see the rising steam. It was a magical place.

And then I was ill. I felt humiliated and a thorough nuisance but thankful that I was in a civilized household with modern remedies and no-one injected me with camphor, morphia or quinine. When the worst of the sickness was over they carried my bed out onto the veranda where Kimani's wife, Mary, came at regular intervals to wring her hands and say, "Memsahib, poor Memsahib," over and over again, and everyone else ran round offering me things I didn't want. What's an African tummy bug compared with those ladies who had travelled on whilst suffering agonizing pains. Freya Stark had contemplated death, she was probably near it, I contemplated death and probably wasn't. Where was my pioneering spirit?

I began to recover. Bill and Dorothy arrived, Dorothy had been a nurse and was sure I would be better under her care. I had the feeling that Paula was annoyed. It was nearing Christmas and we had been invited to their barbecue.

"We'll come to the barbecue and I'll leave her behind," said Paula, making me feel like lost luggage. To me, later, she said, "Don't stay long, you'll find them very stuffy."

Stuffy was, perhaps, the right word for Bill put away vast amounts of food. I began to wonder after one of Dorothy's magnificent meals if this was the best place for convalescence. Neither Paula nor I were big eaters and I marvelled now at this lush gluttony. I still feel it is out of place in a country where so many go hungry.

Bill and Dorothy set out to show me the local sights and I had a good time with them, we visited nearer spots such as Blue Posts and Thika but where oh where were the Flame Trees?

We visited Theatres with African Dancing. "It's too set and put on for tourists," said Paula when she heard.

My favourite trip with them was a visit to the tea growing areas, watching the pluckers and visiting the factory. It smelt and a lot of it went on the floor, I've been a bit fussy about tea ever since I saw its production and wondered what happened to the sweepings.

I didn't find Bill and Dorothy stuffy, a little conventional perhaps, but I forgot my internal troubles and someone had to carry me over the swamp and cure the fever!

On the day I realized I was well again Paula turned up.

"We're going down to the coast," she announced.

"Since when?" I was about to ask but caught her eye and refrained. Instead I went and packed and said, 'Goodbyes' and 'Thank-yous'.

"You can't spend your short time here lying on a couch being fattened up by Dorothy," unsympathetically I thought.

"I thought I'd give you a break," I replied.

"When I want a break I'll let you know, what I want now is a break by the coast, how about you?"

"When do we go?" I asked.

"Tomorrow," she replied, "We'll take our camping things, it's a long drive down so we can have a night in the Tsavo on the way."

We started early, I'd wanted to go on the train but we needed equipment and it was easier to leave it in the back of the little safari car. I knew very little about the Tsavo except that the elephants were said to be red owing to the fact that they rolled and played in the red mud.

There was a good self-help camp here and we saw a magnificent herd of elephants - definitely red. It was a lonely spot and on my own I would surely have got lost. We also saw Kilimanjaro, a beautiful snow-capped peak rising from the plains below. It all looked so peaceful but two quiet lions regarding us from a rock reminded me that this was not a tame country.

On the road nearer to the coast I saw my first Baobab tree. It is an amazing tree, so chunky and smooth, it does look a bit as if its roots are in the air, it's a useful tree with edible leaves and fruit. I was getting more used to Kenyan trees and flowers now, these days they can all be bought in the nearest garden centre, but I have never seen a Baobab. It's a splendid tree.

I was glad to see Mombasa.

"I'm tired of animals," Amanda had written after receiving all my postcards depicting every animal I'd seen, "Please send me pictures of buildings."

Well - here were buildings to delight anyone's heart, showing a much more Eastern style, some very old like Fort Jesus. The buildings here were worth exploring.

Here also was the Indian Ocean, warm and inviting.

We drove north as Paula wanted to visit another archaeological site called Gedi, this was a ruined town now overgrown with trees. We hoped to find a not too expensive hotel near to Malindi for our first night. It was dusk when we found one with an available chalet right on the beach between the whispering palms. The plumbing was a bit doubtful but two resourceful women soon put it to rights. It is easier to do this than to make a fuss and then still find it doesn't work.

Hunger sent us to the main block, so dressed in our long garments again, (a cover-up is the best protection from mosquitos) we went towards what sounded like music. We had hit on the hotel's 'African Night' with dancing and a great help-yourself feast with almost every available dish. It was magnificent, we were all expected to join in the exciting dances and it was dark enough to hide my advancing years.

I felt quite young again. However much I told myself it was all put on for tourists I still enjoyed it, we danced and ate and danced again and when tired out drifted through the palms treading the warm sand while listening to the gentle lapping of the waves on the beach. I slept well.

Breakfast seemed rather flat after all that, and the cornflakes were soggy. I was amused when a helpful waiter appeared at my side and explained to me how to eat them, "with milk and sugar in a plate."

We didn't hurry away, this wasn't a hurrying sort of place.

Paula had the key to a friend's basic cottage along this part of the coast, searching through my notes and diary I can find no mention of where it was, perhaps I never knew, Paula had places she wanted to visit and I wanted to settle down and acquire the sort of tan to make my friends back home envious. We had all we needed with us and I was able to wander about, swim and enjoy the sun. In the sand I found pieces of pink coral and collected enough to make a small necklace for my granddaughter Vicky.

It couldn't last of course, and the day came when Paula decided she had to return.

"I wanted to go South as well," she said, "but we'll do that next time!"

I certainly hoped there would be a next time but now it was back to Nairobi.

I liked Nairobi, it is a pleasant town with plenty of flowering trees and shrubs, my favourite was the Jacaranda, a beautiful tree with blue blossoms. It pleased me that I was beginning to recognize and feel at home with African plants.

There are many interesting buildings too, old ones that I hope won't all be knocked down in order to build lovely new concrete ones. I was alarmed by the crooked wooden scaffolding, it looked very rickety to me, none of the pieces were straight. I suppose it was safe, I never saw any collapse.

Before coming out I'd had the sense to obtain an International driving licence. If we were on a long trip we could share the driving or, if Paula was working, I could borrow her car. Luckily for me Kenya drives on the left and although I had several near misses I managed to avoid a mishap.

I wanted to do some shopping, mainly for presents to take back. I found some fascinating side streets were most of the shops seemed to be run by Asians. In one street, called I think Mokhar Daddah Street, I found nearly everything I needed, I also found the market where I bought some good cheerful batiks very reasonably priced and a lovely big basket which I assured myself I needed to put everything in. I clutched my bag to me most of the time having been warned that it would be easy to lose it in the crush that would surround me. There were street sellers too who were willing to bargain. "Never pay the price asked," said Paula.

Yes, it's an alive place with friendly people, how I wish though that I had been here in earlier years, I don't want the Nairobi of today, I want yesterday. I want bullock carts, dusty safari groups collecting by the Norfolk Hotel. We did have coffee at this historic meeting place and I tried to feel the atmosphere of old, not quite the same after fighting for a parking space. Nairobi had to change of course, it is now a fine bustling town and I didn't see one bullock cart.

CHAPTER 3

"Did you ever hear of someone winning a competition for naming a hotel?" I asked Paula, "The name 'Outspan' won and the prize was champagne."

"I've heard the story," agreed Paula "I believe it was a Grace Barry but I'm not sure if it was a bottle or a case."

"She was the grandmother of a friend of mine, the champagne is irrelevant. I wondered if there was a chance of seeing the place."

"Why not?" Paula sounded enthusiastic. "The town is Nyeri, we could go up to 'Treetops'." It's Mount Kenya country, I have been up it, not this time perhaps but you certainly ought to see it."

At this point she wandered off and I heard taps running, she was still talking and later I was to regret not having listened. I thought I heard the words 'truck' and 'friend' and 'Turkana'. Wasn't this the new name for the Jade Sea. I was dreaming again and buried in my map. When she reappeared with her head wrapped in a towel I surfaced and asked "Not you to Turkana?"

"Not me, someone's friend, are you interested?"

"Count me in."

"Right, I'll get them to book, it's not till next week so we'll do 'Treetops' as soon as we can."

"We're in luck," said Paula, returning from answering a phone call, "You'll never guess. A Chinese delegation is going up and they need some PR. They may be travel agents plugging Kenya for the

Chinese. So get packing, it's for tomorrow and we've been allocated a room." We definitely were in luck.

We drove to Nyeri and the Outspan next morning. The hotel looked solid and spacious, it had lovely gardens, we had lunch there and I had time to wander round. I wanted to see the town too, for Baden-Powell's house 'Paxta' is there and as a one time Akela with my village cub pack I thought this essential. I had also promised to put flowers on my friend's mother's grave. Paula took photos of my doing so though I'm sure my friend didn't need proof. Then we went up to Treetops with an armed hunter, fortunately we saw nothing that he felt he had to shoot. The hotel is built on high tree stumps and props, it isn't the original hotel which was burnt down in the Mau Mau troubles but a larger version still at the same level so that animals can pass underneath. I was fascinated by the sight of a large animated bath rug passing beneath us. A nearby pool attracted many animals and I saw Rhino in the distance among the trees.

Paula joined me and the Chinese arrived, I am in all their photographs!

"You'll enjoy the dinner," Paula said, "I've seen the menu, there's nothing there you don't like."

"What about the Chinese?" I asked, "Has anyone consulted them? I bet they're all vegetarian?"

These casual remarks caused consternation. They were and no-one had consulted them. It was lucky that Paula managed to convey this odd whim to a meat loving staff. Enough suitable fare was found to provide them with a satisfactory meal.

In the night we were woken by the cry "Elephant" and we all (or nearly all, Paula didn't stir) trooped down to the observation room. I heard one guest remark "It's almost as good as television."

At 2am the thought struck me that after all I could have stayed at home but nothing the television could do would make up for the shaking of the building as the elephants rubbed against the supporting stumps. This is the thrill of 'Treetops', being part of the animal world, without vehicles and without the noise of the outside world. The trappings of civilization are with you admittedly, a good meal, a comfortable bed, people to make the stay a pleasant one but the main attractions are the isolation, the peace and the wonderful variety of unafraid animals.

I can't leave 'Treetops' without telling you that Princess

Elizabeth was here when the news came of her father's death. She came as a Princess and left as a Queen.

Guilt was beginning to steal over me. This wonderful and often luxurious holiday wasn't at all to be compared with the travels of my friends the adventurous, literary ladies. It wasn't what I'd had in mind at all, so perhaps this truck trip would make me feel better, especially as it sounded more rugged and more in keeping with the sufferings of earlier days.

The truck left Nairobi in the early dawn.

Sleepily I asked Paula, "Who is this friend of a friend? What's her name and what does she look like?"

"You never listen," replied Paula crossly, "I've never met him, I think his name is Gordon."

I hadn't listened, my mind had been on the adventure on the Jade Sea, on higher things.

"Oh, Paula," I thought, "What have you let me in for!" I was too taken aback to talk.

So here I was with a small and motley crew, an unexpected male, a far from comfortable truck and a great deal of dust. This, after all, was more of the sort of thing I had in mind. I had many misgivings when it came to the test but also a certain feeling of relief. It would be something to boast about. Paula drove off and left me to my fate.

We were a strange collection of some twenty people looking at each other suspiciously, most were in couples, one or two singles but I couldn't see a lone male except a youth of about 18 and I didn't think Paula's friend would be this young. We boarded the truck. Jim was the owner driver and he and a relief driver-odd job man sat in front along with the cook, everyone paired up for the twin seats, I sat alone. At the last minute a tall military looking man arrived, took a look round and, raising a rather battered looking hat, joined me.

"Gordon, I presume?" I asked in a Stanley-Livingstone sort of way.

"And you must be Joy."

I admitted it.

We got on fairly well, the trouble was he didn't seem to like people very much and, although polite to me, managed in a very short while to make himself unpopular with everyone else. He had his good and useful points, he was a fluent Swahili speaker and an excellent bargainer if we stopped to admire and were immediately surrounded by traders. Beads, bananas or stones he always knew the exact price we should pay. He was not at all keen on work and explained to me in a very reasonable way that there were plenty of other people to do it. We had a long way to go and if we didn't linger over the stops for wood gathering or meals, we could make good progress. So everyone was expected to, and did, help. Except Gordon.

By night-time we were a united group and mostly anti-Gordon. I found myself making excuses for him and then I realized that everyone thought we were a couple, I felt curiously enough, protective towards him, there must be some reason I told myself, for his odd unsocial behaviour. He had many good points as I found out. He could pick up scorpions without them harming him and he had perfected that wonderful drawn out "eeeeeeeee" used by the local inhabitants to precede an utterance.

We had a very civilized camp at Samburu by the river. Tents were handed out.

"Where shall we put ours?" asked Gordon.

Nonplussed for a moment I hesitated long enough for an American called Barbara to rush in. No doubt she felt she was saving me from a fate worse than death, or she could have singled me out as the only possible partner. Thinnish, cleanish, motherly looking, perhaps I was, no doubt she had already seen the size of the tents. She almost dragged me to the site she had chosen, I gave Gordon an apologetic grin and wondered what Tom would have said. Nothing perhaps, just shot him.

Barbara proved to be a strict disciplinarian, we were first up with out tent every evening and the first to pack it away in the morning, we were first at mealtimes and first away to bed, she kept me tidily in my section of the tent and told me exactly where to stow my things. Gordon was left to fend for himself, he bore me no ill will for this desertion.

"Perhaps you are right" he muttered as he wandered off although I hadn't said a word. Gordon would have been more fun than my American friend and Tom need never have known.

The lone youth and Gordon eventually teamed up, the youth was energetic and willing to be left to do the double share so all were satisfied.

How I wished that first night that I had brought a blow-up mattress, those supplied were very thin and I had a sleepless night. Alas for my desire for simplicity. I crawled (almost) into the nearby lodge to have a secret wash and a coffee with Gordon.

I appreciated him on the second night as I found myself with another mattress, double my rights, this one belonged to the cook who was demanding his. No-one let on.

"He doesn't need one," said Gordon who was retaliating as the standard of cooking was not to his liking. "And you need to sleep."

I slept well and my conscience didn't worry me.

A strange man, Gordon, a mixture of racial prejudices, sarcasm and kindness.

Another passenger who was not popular except in the daytime was a Danish girl. She snored. Her snores rocked the encampment at night and most of us watched where she pitched her tent before moving as far away as possible and still keep within the group. Nobody offered to share with her, perhaps she did it on purpose.

In the evenings after the fire was lit, we put up the benches and gathered round for supper. No-one sat up late, Jim insisted on an early start. In the morning the fire was blown up again, a simple breakfast, break camp and we were off again.

Our camping spots became wilder and wilder. No latrines were built, they weren't considered necessary. We had no trouble in these deserted sites with the normal expectant sightseers. None of the Victorian ladies mention the problem of body waste removal. Perhaps with all that clothing it wasn't one, a thick long skirt can be protective in more ways than one. As I wondered off into the bush my only possible companion was a Honey Bear whose hole was adjacent to my chosen spot.

It was a rough journey becoming hotter and dustier as we travelled North towards the lake, the scenery changed and here it was jagged, dry, grey and volcanic. Then as a contrast we came upon this wonderful Jade Sea. It really is this lovely colour, we drove alongside for some miles and then camped beside it. My spirits rose, this was a real safari, an unusual place even if it was only a truck and not camels.

I've never liked camels, they were, I thought, scruffy and they spat. It was not until years later, in Pakistan, that I changed my mind about them and saw what magnificent beasts they were.

It could not be called a sandy beach where we now camped, there were trees which broke the line of grey barren shore. It was not easy to put up the tents but we had wood there as well as that we had piled on the truck roof. There were distant mountains, it didn't look the slightest bit like travel agents' guides to Paradise. It was bliss to me.

I knew then that this was what I had come to see, wide open desert like spaces. As different as it could be from our gentle Dorset countryside. I slept well.

In the night it rained, it soaked everything, it hadn't rained for three years and we were, therefore, very well received by the local inhabitants as obvious, saintly rain bringers.

We were able to buy fish at a nearby village occupied by a fish eating people willing to show us their simple round grass huts and their nearby acquired school. This lake fish was very good indeed cooked on our camp fire. I have a feeling that we had chips with it. Gordon complained that he didn't eat fish but no-one took much notice except to demand his share.

Gordon reminded me of Isabella Bird's Major Herbert Sawyer whom she calls the 'Sahib', she travelled with him from Baghdad to Teheran. I started to think of Gordon as the 'Major', I was only with him for a short time whereas Isabella bore with Sawyer's similar behaviour for many weeks. I now felt I had something more in common with Isabella other than the fact that we had both started our travels at a mature time of life. I still knew, though, that I had nothing in common with the stamina, deprivations, discomforts and amazing endurance of the remarkable Victorian lady travellers. They all wrote so cheerfully of their experiences, they all suffered in some way or other but they made light of their illnesses and sufferings. I now admired them even more.

No old-time traveller could have been dustier than we were, the canvas shields on the truck sides were up so that we could see the surrounding countryside. Only in a dust storm or if bees attacked us would they be lowered.

Water had been limited, we all had an unkempt, earthy look. The lake shimmered before us, water was now unlimited.

I waited awhile, determined to have all this wetness to myself, a swim in it and a very good wash, the others went in different directions and I set off towards the wonderful colour of the lake.

Talk of crocs did not deter me. At last I had the feel of a vast, great wilderness.

I heard steps behind, I felt a moment of unease almost panic but, on turning, there was the 'Major' in swimming trunks with a towel over his shoulder and I felt all the solitude of Brighton Beach. I abandoned ideas of stripping off and a long soak but was pleased with myself for having the foresight to put on my very smart bikini and reassured myself that I was safe now and he could protect me from the rumoured crocodiles. We saw none.

We had a good refreshing cup of tea organized by Gordon on our return, tea wasn't on the menu at that hour but if Gordon ordered tea - tea arrived.

Barbara arrived shortly afterwards having been on a different jaunt, a tough walk I feel sure. I felt her disapproval of my slack and improper behaviour but she made no remark. She couldn't understand my curious friendship with the misanthropic Gordon. She could tell me her troubles, and I could fall asleep listening, in the tent at night. As she hadn't invited me to America I had no intention of seeing her again when the trip was over.

We returned to Nairobi by a different route and ran out of food. The bread had a greenish tinge that I didn't fancy. We had plenty of bananas, no-one complained. Gordon would have done so but by then he was suffering from a tummy bug and was unusually silent. Only I knew of his malady, everyone being under the impression that he was suffering the pangs of love and was in distress as we approached the final parting. This did wonders for my morale so I didn't disillusion them.

Our camp was beside a beautiful small clear pool fed by a spring. We all took the opportunity to have a swim and thorough wash. Except Gordon. He didn't fancy sharing this facility with all the 'riffraff'. He was ignored, he strode off and the party looked knowingly at each other and at me.

At the last camp we were back on the main road and at Samburu again. A party of Australians were camping near us and our men noticed a girl from their camp lying and relaxing in the river, in viewing distance not only of ourselves, but of various large crocodiles. Our men rushed down shouting and waving their arms but she was quite unperturbed saying that she couldn't see any and they were scaremongers. We could see an extra large reptile slithering down from the opposite bank. She moved. It was a good conversation point around our camp fire.

We only had one theft on the whole trip, it was here at Samburu and instead of blaming native thieves we were sure it was taken by this Australian group. We appeared to have taken a dislike to them perhaps because no-one said 'Thankyou' for saving the life of one of their members. There was no fraternization, it was very much 'us' and 'them'. We had been together long enough to feel ourselves as one.

Paula met the truck in Nairobi and the group scattered and lost its identity. I was too tired to talk, I felt like sleeping for a week.

I think the cook got the sack at the end of the trip, I know I over-tipped him. I was feeling guilty over the extra mattress that mysteriously appeared in our tent every evening. Unnecessarily guilty as there were only 19 in the party and twenty mattresses and Gordon was right in thinking that one was not earmarked for the cook. The remembrance of the tip stayed with him for he was waiting for me six years later in Kenyatta Avenue. He greeted me as a long lost relative. Simon was with me at the time.

"You do have some funny friends," he said.

The end was now in sight, Paula was still muttering about Amboseli.

"Kilimanjaro is a wonderful sight from there," she mumbled on, "I suppose it will have to be next time."

"But I did see it when we went to the coast, I admit it's wonderful and I have no intention of going up it."

We looked at each other.

"I have to go, you know," I told her. "I have a husband and a family and a garden, added to which I must find a new job and start saving again."

All good things come to an end, I had to organize myself to pack, to do last minute shopping. There were 'goodbyes' to say and many 'Thankyous'.

But I had the travelling bug and nothing now was going to stop me.

CHAPTER 4

It was cold when I landed at Heathrow, a raw feeling I had managed to forget. I shivered all the way home and, next day being market day in our nearest town, set out, not only to replenish stocks (what had Tom been living on?) but to look for the warmest, lined, hooded coat I could find. I had plenty of coats, none of which now seemed adequate. I felt my image had changed too, and basic needs were more important to me than fashionable trends. While deciding between a duffle coat and a keep-snow-and-wind-out type of thick green corduroy, I saw my old colleague, May. She was the only member of staff who had supported me when I decided to end that particular phase of my life. She had gone into the education department of a local prison and was doing well.

"I'm glad I met you," she said in her forthright fashion, "Would you be interested in coming to the prison, there's a vacancy?"

Would I? I'd only been back a day and here was a possible opening.

"I'll see you get a form, the interview is next week so don't hang about!"

I think the main reason I landed the job was because I was willing to work throughout the summer holidays. Other interviewees had already booked theirs and this was not well received by the Head of Education who expected to be away for the whole of August and his Deputy had a young family and hoped for a slack time during their school holidays. Remedial teaching was continuous and went on throughout the year as prisoners' needs arose, they didn't have summer holidays.

I was not better qualified that the other applicants but I was more mature. May told me afterwards that this was also viewed with satisfaction as the departing teacher was considered too sexy and had been accused of 'working up' the men. On such odd qualifications do interviews depend. I once heard that in Victorian times plainer teachers were often selected as the turnover in pretty ones getting married was so great. The main change now is that married teachers are no longer required to leave. All the women teachers here at the prison were married.

Having this new job I had to make a good impression and I did not venture far the following winter. I spent Christmas with Amanda, her husband Michael, George and Vicky.

George returned with me as a friend of his had stayed by himself with his grandmother and he was anxious to make the same experiment. It was only to be for one night but it snowed and we were snowed in. George loved it, we discovered a new white world and tobogganing with a tin tray.

Coming in one day he said anxiously "There's a cat under one of the sheds".

"We haven't a cat, it's more likely to be a rat," I too was worried, I don't like rats.

"I'm sure it's a cat, can I have a saucer of milk?"

I gave him a saucer of milk and he was a watchful frozen lump when I went out to retrieve him.

"It's a tiny kitten, I saw it."

"What colour is it?"

"A sort of battleship grey."

So Battleship joined our household, she was always slightly wild. I remembered that the thatcher, working on our roof before the snow, had said that there was a cat with kittens in a far hedge. She had left this one behind when she had removed them to the safety of a barn and it had taken shelter under one of our sheds. Battleship was a lovely little cat and the beginning of a long line of greys (or blues?) that are with me still. It's an extra problem when I go away for I have to remind Tom to feed them and to leave enough tins in an obvious place.

This time George had full control over the feeding and training of Battleship as I slipped on the ice, sprained my ankle and was put out of action.

As I hobbled around I thought of last year, of the warmth, the barbecues, the golden coast and the sweet smell of Frangipane.

The snow went. Amanda fetched a reluctant George. "No we can't take it home George, we've got three cats," and in the New Year I returned to work. I was saving again.

One of the best ways of saving is not to spend.

"You do without things," Freya Stark once said.

I would do without things. I no longer felt the need for visits to the hairdresser except for an occasional cut. Most of the teachers at the prison wore trousers, discouraged in my last school, and I had plenty of these. I had to have a car to get to work but Tom was willing to keep this on the road for me so that I needn't drive his. The only time mine has any dents in it is when he or Simon borrow it but this sort of argument is always ignored.

* * *

Simon rang.

"I'm off to Nigeria next week."

"Nigeria?" I was both hopeful and fearful, mentally seeing it on the map. West Africa and the White Man's Grave. When my father was offered it he had refused point blank to go there.

"Nigeria," I repeated, "For how long?" And I added apprehensively, "But you've just met this girl."

Just met this girl sounds somewhat dull but I dare not sound too enthusiastic because this wasn't 'this girl' to me, this was 'THE GIRL'. The one I'd always hoped for and the mother of my grandchildren. At that time I hadn't visualized these grandchildren, I just knew Jennie was 'the girl' because I knew Simon. She was full of adventure as well as sound common sense. To be pretty and sympathetic as well seemed almost too much. We simply mustn't lose her.

"She seems an adventurous sort," he now said vaguely, and as I wasn't deceived by his casual approach perhaps he wasn't deceived by mine. "I'll come back and we'll get married."

I thought of some of the others. I'd met the usual assortment of hopefuls, the girl whose father mustn't know where she was, the one whose father rang up nearly every hour to make sure she was in my care, the apple eater, the devout catholic who brought along her uncle priest, the one who couldn't be persuaded to leave mother, the blonde bombshell, and one I quite regretted, a vague artist that he lost somewhere on the Bristol line and we never saw again.

Simon had started off with a medical career in mind. I think he had no idea of what he wanted to do and thought it sounded the sort of thing that appealed to teachers and parents. He was not cut out for medicine at all, he had managed to get into a London hospital but was thrown out in his first term, he was given a very bad report and the warden of his hostel accused him of 'rocketing around."

Simon denied this hotly while trying to convince us and himself that he had left voluntarily.

"It wasn't like that at all, he accused me of flirting with his wife."

"And did you?"

"Oh! Come off it, Mother," he admonished me, "She was so old it was ridiculous."

"Well, how old?"

"She must have been at least thirty."

"The real truth," he went on "Was that he fancied this Au Pair girl and she preferred me."

I preferred not to know any more details though he did say she was 'very knowledgeable and helpful'.

I changed the subject.

"What are you going to do?" I asked.

Tom was angry and I wanted to have some ideas of a future.

"I want to be with things that are alive and healthy, no-one goes to a doctor unless they're ill. I want to be out-of-doors. Why can't I farm?"

"Unless you're qualified, you'll be a farmer's boy all your life, we can't afford to buy you a farm."

"What's wrong with being a farmer's boy?" he asked as he departed moodily and in the direction of our local. This turned out to be a good move as, leaning on the bar, he poured out his troubles to a sympathetic farmer who offered him a job which he immediately accepted. All I insisted upon was day release at our local Farm Institute where he did so well that the Principal persuaded him to go to full time College.

Take heed all despairing parents, on a career he really enjoyed he did well and when I attended his last degree ceremony and saw him scarlet gowned with Tudor hat, pride nearly reduced me to tears.

* * *

So to Nigeria he went after telling us that he'd let us know what it was like.

Jennie was working in London but we kept constantly in touch. One day she rang.

"I've had a telegram," she said, "It says :- 'Can't get back, come out here'. What shall I do?"

I didn't hesitate.

"I'll help you pack." I replied. "In his last letter he said it was very hot so you won't need much."

"I could do with a bit of hotness," she said philosophically. It was the usual cold, damp English early spring.

Simon wrote to me about the ceremony. It didn't sound quite like an English conventional wedding. I was sad I couldn't make it at that time but it took place at the British Consulate so it was all above board and legal. The registrar was an Alhaji, someone who has been to Mecca, he kept them waiting two hours in typical Nigerian fashion and while they got hotter and hotter they started on the Champagne to keep themselves cool, fortunately, I am thankful to say, they were still able to sign the necessary documents. I don't think they bothered with a honeymoon.

"This Christmas I am going to Nigeria," I announced to anyone who would listen.

"My goodness," people said, "You can't go there, it's awful," or "My friend's son went and he couldn't get back fast enough."

I went on saying it, I didn't care, surely it wasn't all bad. I read up about the country, about the Biafran war, about the culture and the people. No longer the white man's grave and my yellow fever inoculation was well within its effective limits. The saving had a purpose again.

Simon and Jennie both wanted a family and they didn't waste much time. Simon wrote to say that Jennie would be coming home to have the baby, he would come with her but they would have to return soon after the baby was born.

"What are you thinking of?" I had managed to get him on the phone. "You can't take a baby to Nigeria."

"Everyone has babies in Nigeria," he replied, "They'll love it."

They came and Elizabeth was born. I couldn't wait for Christmas, I'd hardly seen my new granddaughter.

Just before Christmas a friend of Jennie's called Ann rang me. She was returning to Nigeria and to her boyfriend Patrick. Jennie had suggested we travelled together. It was a great idea. It is easier to travel with someone, it's a nuisance having to drag everything around while getting a cup of tea or going to the loo. If there are two of you, one can mind luggage, it's reassuring too if there are delays or any problems.

We met at the airport, there was a delay and we got to know each other over an unexpected meal. She was small, dark and animated. We got on well.

I was even more glad of the company when we landed at Lagos. I was with someone who knew the ropes, I was glad too that I had been in Africa before, I was not entirely new to the continent and was partly prepared for the shock. Nairobi airport was harmony itself compared to the chaos of Lagos. There were hot, long queues, I should have been entirely lost as nobody seemed to be going anywhere. Everybody suddenly seemed so large and impressive, the western looking passengers had suddenly become a vast Nigerian crowd. I think Ann determinedly pushed me through customs or I should have been there still, she was perfectly happy. It was a jungle scene all right, a jungle of people, luggage and parcels, I had no idea what was where or who was who.

It seemed to me that all Nigeria was contained in this small area, all greeting, shouting, complaining or welcoming. I followed meekly in Ann's wake as she, unperturbed, sailed us both through customs. My peculiar luggage no longer looked so peculiar among the strange assortment of African packages. (Simon had asked for a large umbrella and a barbecue).

Then I saw Simon on the other side of the barriers waiting and waving with the outside world. Patrick was there too, the confusion was over and we were out. Ann and Patrick were reunited and drove off.

I was in Africa again, here the heat really hit me, it flowed through me like turning on a hot shower. I've never been a warm person but here I started shedding clothes even on the way to Simon's truck. How wonderful I thought, to be really warm at last, later I began to think affectionately of cooler climates. This heat was very different from the heat of East Africa, it's an all enveloping heat full of dust and smells and noise.

We drove to a resthouse, it was cooler here and we had it to ourselves. I like the simplicity of these places because I am not a great stuffer of exotic foods. I like eggs on toast, unadulterated dishes, fruit and lots of tea. We were the only guests at the resthouse, there were two men to do cooking and cleaning, both helpful and friendly, very different from the officials at the airport.

"Do you want to see Lagos?" Simon asked.

I thought driving through that I had seen enough of it to last me a lifetime, but Simon had shopping to do and I agreed to take part in this exercise, besides I wanted to change some money. Simon was very vague about this just saying something about "Leave it to me." I thought it best not to enquire too deeply into the matter, this was not Kenya. Things did seem to be extraordinarily expensive, perhaps the official rate of exchange was unrealistic.

Shopping here was necessary as there was a shortage of certain goods up country where Simon was based. So we drove around Lagos and I decided that it was not my sort of town.

Once, years ago, when I was in my early teens and suffering from a bout of 'flu, I found among my father's books one entitled 'The Bight of Benin'. This was not a geographical book but a volume of short stories and it had impressed me with its atmosphere of sticky heat. I don't remember any plots, as far as I can remember it consisted of people sitting around complaining of the heat and sweating profusely on a waterfront. I felt the heat but the deserted waterfront was no more, this was a vast bustling, crowded town. Why did this book make such an impression me I wonder, perhaps it was a cold, foggy spell in winter and the contrast appealed to me.

Generally I like African towns, I am used to the disintegrating roads, the red dust, the overcrowded shacks and broken pavements full of rubbish but Lagos seemed worse than Nairobi or Mombasa, it was an extended version of the airport only more ramshackle and potholed. I was told that there were some good areas but we didn't visit them and my first impressions were of the rush and noise.

I slept well that night at the rest house and next morning we drove north. It was a good road but all roads in Nigeria are not so good. Others have written about the roads in Nigeria, my first impressions were that they were not too bad, an occasional pot-hole being avoidable. Later I saw horrifying accidents and these and other roads I will mention when they are in the right place in my narrative.

We passed through Ibadan which looked like a rusty, red, tin-shack town with a seemingly endless mass of corrugated roofs interspersed with an occasional palm tree. Simon assured me that there were good shops here, but he said cars could only go out on alternate days according to the last digit on the number plate, there were odd and even days. The traffic was so heavy this was necessary but even then the town was blocked up solid by about nine o'clock.

"Another time," I said somewhat daunted. In any case I wanted to see Jennie and Elizabeth.

"We could all come when I have a conference at IITA," he said. "I shall have to come in a week or two, you'll enjoy it and it will be a break for Jennie."

We passed this place, the International Institute for Tropical Agriculture, it looked like a green park amid all the ramshackle buildings of the town beyond it. I looked forward to the visit.

Ann and Patrick, having no shopping to do, had arrived at the Bungalow before us. They were staying until after Christmas, it was now December 24th, and then going to their own house in Kano.

The bungalow was built on the system of build-a-bit and then-build-on-a-bit-more-when-required system. So at one end was a kitchen and living room and the various bedrooms were down a long passage. Simon and Jennie occupied the one at the very end. It was bigger as it lost nothing to the passage. The site of the bungalow was within a compound with other similar bungalows, the whole marked with a large notice 'Chicken Farm'; it belonged to them I understood, though how they managed to run three cars on the proceeds of the farm when there were no chickens and no eggs was a mystery, even though petrol was only 30p per gallon. Perhaps on the rents from the bungalows or maybe it was one of those industries that do better without the actual product. We were handed a chicken on Christmas Day so perhaps there were some elsewhere. As this bird was alive and kicking we didn't fancy it as a meal so Simon made it a little run hoping it might eventually lay some eggs.

It was a great welcome here and lovely to see Jennie and the baby again. Among my things were Christmas decorations, unobtainable here, pudding and all sorts of odds and ends for tomorrow's festivities. We had a grand unpacking.

That evening there was a party somewhere and Simon and Jennie were going, I was asked but decided on a quiet evening at home. Elizabeth was a peaceful baby and Jennie had got into the habit of taking her around. I could unpack, settle myself in and generally relax, there was a magardi or guard and a large dog to keep me company. A bitch as it turned out, as it proceeded to have puppies, an event I was not prepared for and I had no idea where Simon was. The lights went out. The magardi appeared with a torch saying "Nepa". I had no idea what this meant, thinking it to be in some tribal language. Later I understood it to mean 'Nigerian Electric Power', something or other. Everyone cried out 'Nepa' as soon as the power failed which was frequently, usually when a meal was being cooked, in the heat of the day when air-conditioning was essential or in the evening when the lights were needed. What I didn't know this first evening was that there was a generator. The magardi stood grinning at me probably expecting me to start it up. I groped my way to my room where I had a torch and then searched for candles. I couldn't find any and I was unsure of the availability of batteries. By noises, the dog seemed to be able to cope. There are times when it is best to surrender to circumstances, this was one of them; I went to bed.

Without the air-conditioning it was hot, mosquito nets were essential here and under the net it seemed airless, I lay on the bed sweating.

Later when the family returned Simon started up the generator and I wondered if it was better to suffer the noise it made or the heat of a Nigerian night. The lights came on so I rejoined family life.

"That dog's had puppies," I announced accusingly.

"How many?" Simon sounded anxious for his dog I thought, not for me.

"How should I know, it was pitch black, I decided it was her affair."

He rushed to her.

"Six," he proclaimed triumphantly.

What I didn't know was that this happy event had been eagerly anticipated by many families especially those with children, for these were the progeny of a good guard dog. next day, news having spread, we had a stream of visitors anxious to book a puppy.

Extract from a letter to Tom, found later among his correspondence and which has served as a useful memory prompter.

"Someone is coming home on Sunday and will post this to you in the UK. This seems the safest way as there is some doubt as to the reliability of the Nigerian post. There are various stories as to what happens to it here. One theory is that everything over a certain weight is automatically burned. Postcards disappear because of the pictures so mine might not arrive. Aerogrammes are the safest I'm told, but of course they don't appear to be available.

Jennie's car hasn't turned up yet but we hope it will come soon as it will make us more independent. So far we have to rely on others or borrow a project car with driver if one is available. We had a trip with one of Simon's team yesterday but it was not a great success, it will be better when we can go on our own.

You will be pleased to hear that the seeds I brought out have not been wasted. Jennie and I have managed to make a small vegetable garden at the back of the bungalow and a few things are already coming up. Simon has netted it as his dog has six puppies. We water it by a canal system from the kitchen and bathrooms. Simon has planted a lawn with grass plants called Bermudan grass, it isn't quite like an English lawn but it may improve and it does keep the red soil out of the house. Simon talks of a rockery but I think we must be content with humbler projects. As yet I know none of the trees, shrubs or birds around here.

The friend bringing this letter is called Lydia Parker, she is bringing her two children back to school. They spent Christmas Day with us, I didn't much like these children, a boy of fourteen and a girl of twelve, I thought them bumptious and self-opinionated but I shan't see them again anyway so it doesn't really matter. The father, Roy, is the economist of the team - a large quiet man very different from his children.

The team manager is away at the moment, I think he should be back next week. His wife isn't with him. I've not met everyone on the team yet but one couple, Ian and Fran with two young boys, I like very much.

The town is higgledy-piggledy with the same contrasts as in other African towns. The centre is dusty, full of people and various vehicles good and bad. Also it is hot. The outskirts are either overcrowded or tree-lined and spacious. There is, believe it or not, a garden centre but we haven't visited it yet so I don't know if there are any plants. On the other side of the town is a big market, it looks interesting and I shall suggest we go there when Jeannie's car comes.

I have managed to get my Visa extended, this should be an easy task but the officials in offices are so rude. This is strange because as a people the Nigerians are delightful, friendly, happy and fond of children. The best thing perhaps would be to take the baby along, I'll try it next time. Just a tiny bit of power seems to go to their heads. Perhaps they don't know how offensive they are, I wish someone would tell them how very unprofessional it is. One was on the phone to his girlfriend and totally ignored our presence - a screaming baby would have helped! I wonder if there is a school of discourteous behaviour or if they merely copy each other.

Elizabeth is a lovely baby and seems content even in the heat, she swims nightly in her bath but swimming is definitely not for me. Just after Christmas we all went to the local hotel which has a so-called swimming pool. You should have seen it! A scummy, murky green, which I refused to enter in spite of the scornful taunting of the Parker children. I felt justified when I was the only one not to develop a nasty septic throat. Rumour had it that a small body had been recovered from the bottom of the pool, it must have been there for some days. I am not sure of the authenticity of the story but it wouldn't surprise me if it was true. Nothing could be seen of the bottom through that dark grotty mess. A man stood by with a whip all the time we were there and probably when we weren't, assumably to keep the small boys within their depth as he flicked the whip over them when they ventured out into the deep end. Or what was probably the deep end. I thought of our local lido and wished we could transplant it here.

Our houseman, Sammy, cooked a Nigerian meal for us the other day. Usually Jennie does the cooking or Sammy does it under her supervision. I can't say I like Nigerian food, one dish was so powerful it lifted the roof off my mouth, the other so tasteless that to me it was inedible. The idea with these two dishes is to eat them alternately. Give me fish and chips every time. The tasteless dish is pounded yam, we hear this pounding endlessly from neighbouring houses. I can hear the thump, thump, thump going on most of the day. I went over with my camera to the bungalow opposite and asked if I might take a photograph, I suppose I looked as strange to them as they did to me, but they posed, picked their noses and stared and stared.

An interesting vegetable or fruit here is plantain, it's the same family as the banana which is what I thought it was as it looks exactly like one. It isn't sweet though, but is fine fried with bacon. We were offered apples the other day at the stall but at one pound each decided we could do without.

Simon is talking of going on a Safari next week, we are looking forward to this but are not at all sure what to expect."

I re-read this and it all comes back to me.

CHAPTER 5

That first morning I awoke as a lanky self-possessed young man opened my door and came in.

"Who are you?" I asked resolving to lock my door in future.

"I'm Neil," he answered in a you-should-know-who-I-am sort of voice.

"Hello and Goodbye Neil. Shut the door as you go out."

He withdrew and I heard him go down the corridor and open Simon and Jennie's door as he had mine. He retreated at great speed and some language followed him down the passage which included some words no son of mine should have known. Simon isn't often angry, what can they have been up to?

Neil was only one of a curious assortment of team members. The team leader was away so I had yet to meet him. Lydia and Roy arrived next to make my acquaintance and to stay for Christmas celebrations. Roy was big, cheerful and bouncy, Lydia small, bouncy and officious. I didn't like their children.

Another young couple were Norman and Megan with their small son Lloyd. Megan always had her head in a book, she seemed to take no interest in the outside world although she occasionally looked up to tell Lloyd 'not to'. He took little notice, why should he when she never followed this up but plunged straight back into her book world. There was something ostentatious about it and superior as if we lesser folk were of no importance. The child seemed to survive, others rescued him from various dangerous situations, often this was Norman in a drowsy sort of way.

Norman was the young man who offered to take us on the trip I had mentioned to Tom in my letter as not being a success. This was putting it mildly.

The outing was to view a site on which the project's new town was to be built. Up to now everyone was scattered in an assortment of houses, only the furniture was the same in each. We accepted the offer of this outing, the site was some way away and would last for several hours.

"Fine," said Jennie, "We shall enjoy it, what shall I bring?"

Norman replied that he would bring everything.

We were delighted and looked forward to a picnic lunch. The party consisted of Norman, Lloyd, Jennie, Elizabeth and myself.

The trouble with the journey there was that Norman had no idea of the way. He was the sort that would never admit to ignorance, he had to know best, and kept telling the driver instead of asking. The driver, who did know the way, was obviously enjoying Norman's discomfort. "You said this way - Sur," as he landed us in a very bushy obvious cul-de-sac. As far as we were concerned we were lost but the driver got out, disappeared into the bush, and returned with cigarettes and titbits for himself so it appeared that he wasn't. He was determined and who could blame him to do exactly as he was told even if we were all stuck there all night. It was not until Jennie, sizing up the situation and knowing the driver, suggested that we just drove straight there. With a grin and a wink he did so. Even then Norman would not admit that he had been wrong.

We arrived at the village nearest to the wired in site and caused great excitement as the red-headed baby was sighted. Jennie held her up to delighted cries and hand clapping. We looked at the site but had no means of getting in as Norman had no keys.

We should now have the picnic and Norman produced a bottle of water. We stared in disbelief. I know that this is a precious commodity and I tried to be appreciative but I, along with Jennie, had had a light breakfast and had been looking forward to a treat provided by someone else. We could have brought something, we had asked and Jennie especially, who was still feeding Elizabeth, needed reinforcement. Elizabeth was the only one satisfied.

However nothing was said, Jennie and I looked at each other, we drank our water, tried to pretend it was wine, suggested we'd seen enough of the place, thank you very much and could we go home. I tried to think philosophically on the way home but I think more philosophically with a cup of tea and a bit of home made cake.

The return journey was greatly improved as Jennie had a quiet word with the driver who gave her a conspiratorial smile and drove the quickest way home. Nobody spoke. Once home I quickly put the kettle on and we settled down to refreshments and a quiet dissection of Norman's character.

"That Norman!" said Simon when we told him. I know he never said anything to Norman but he did to the driver.

"You can do that to Mr Norman if you wish but never, never, never to my wife and Mother ..." 'Or Else' was understood. The driver was not subdued, he went off grinning. Was this Nigerian humour?

Although we hadn't lingered at the site I had seen enough to be a little doubtful of its having been properly surveyed. I voiced my doubts to Simon.

"Have you any plans of the place?" I asked, "The sort of thing a surveyor would do. I wouldn't mind going again with someone who knows the way and carrying a little sustenance."

He brought the plans, he'd had his doubts too. We studied them together and on Simon's next free day we drove there.

Villagers again came out to look us over, this time approaching nearer. I wondered what would happen here and to them if this settlement became reality. I don't think it ever did. A pity, they were careful, pleasing plans with big bungalows all arranged around a fine swimming pool. They had good gardens too, all on solid rock, perhaps it was better than a swamp. I was now convinced that the plans had been drawn up in an office without reference to the site or geological formation. Easy enough, given the site size, to imagine this attractive place and produce these delightful plans.

"The old man is back," said Simon, referring to the project manager. "He wants to give a dinner party. You can, if you like, reinforce my suggestion that the project needs a geologist."

It was a good and lively dinner party but I was not impressed with the old man.

"Call me Clem," he said in what I thought was a condescending manner. His name was Clement Wainwright, he was not my cup of tea. I thought he expected and received a certain amount of deference and as Simon would never kowtow he would not be the most favoured member of the team in the old man's eyes. I suppose I was thus prejudiced against him from the start but I felt he was superficial and later I suspected a penchant for little girls. However this has nothing to do with my story and on the evening of the dinner party he was in an attentive mood when we suggested that the project could do with a good geologist, preferably one used to Nigerian ways.

Jennie's car arrived at last, it was a good bright orange, easy to manage with big wheels and room to accommodate the folding pram.

"Can we go to the market?" was my first request. My feet were hot and I wanted to buy some flip-flops, everyone wore them

"I don't see why not," said Jennie.

"No, no," said Sammy who was standing by and as in all Africa, cheerfully, unashamedly and openly listening.

"Why no, no?" asked Jennie, "We go now, now."

"Then I come too, many rough people."

"We surely don't need Sammy, do we?" I asked Jennie, "Can't we go on our own and take Elizabeth in the pram?"

"Let's try," said Jennie.

We folded the pram, put it in the back and set off.

The market looked fun, full of colour and cheerfully dressed people, there seemed to be a predominance of plastic but otherwise plenty of interesting looking stalls. There was, unlike home, plenty of space for parking, so after parking and reassembling the pram we put Elizabeth in it and started off.

The crown gathered so slowly we hardly noticed it at first, it was just a few children trailing along and occasionally peeping at the red-headed baby in its own little carriage. But a red-headed baby in its own little carriage was a rare sight in a mid-Nigerian town and more children gathered to see the fun. Once a nucleus had formed it gathered momentum, became a large crowd and movement of the pram was difficult.

It was entirely halted when an old Indian woman went down

on her knees and appeared to be praying.

Jennie and I agreed to abandon ideas of a lovely shopping spree in the market. It was not, after all, much like that in our local town.

I was taken by surprise by the harmless inquisitiveness, I had not realized that we should be something of a spectacle, something so extraordinary to these people who merely wanted to look at so strange a sight. It was almost going back to the experiences of early travellers but whereas it was difficult for them to get away from the embarrassment, once we and the crowds managed to get to the car, we drove off and left them.

When we returned there was Sammy with a very I-told-you-so expression.

"Next time, I come," he said firmly.

Sammy loved a little diversion and I wondered what his role would have been. Policing perhaps, a director of traffic or a promoter of unusual sights.

I bought my flip-flops from a trader at the side of the road, it was whilst buying these that a boy approached us with apples as I mentioned in my letter to Tom.

"Do you want some?" asked Jennie as we looked at the shrivelled specimens.

"Some?" I queried, "Not even one if my calculations of the currency are correct and they cost £1 each. I can well do without."

I could see no point when there are such good local fruits about, mango, pawpaw and bananas. I could wait until I reached home to enjoy a good cox when I knew it would taste magnificent.

I mentioned Plantain in my letter to Tom, I'd read about it as the traveller Mary Kingsley mentions it. As I had always imagined it as a relation to our own plantain with bigger leaves and perhaps eaten like spinach, I was surprised to see that it was a relation of the banana. This made sense of Mary Kingsley's description "picked while green and the rind peeled off". She peaks of a "tasteless woolly interior" and I agree with her. Well spiced it's probably palatable, it was reasonable fried with bacon and usefully satisfying.

We were invited to a party with a family called Fraser, the mother was a doctor, I never discovered what her husband did. This was a lunch-time 'picnic' party at their house, I admired the way people could cater for so many with so little, this little would be made to look a lot interspersed with slices of water melon and bits of avocado.

Someone had told Doctor Jane Fraser that I worked in a prison, she was interested and asked me if I should like to visit a Nigerian prison. She offered to introduce me to a priest she knew called Father O'Leary who might be prepared to show me over the local jail. We visited this Father two days later and he agreed, rather reluctantly, to do so. A woman came while we were there carrying a sickle-cell anaemic baby, she came for the Father's blessing as it was not expected to live long. It can't have weighed more than a pound or two and she carried it wrapped in a piece of cloth like a tiny doll. Jane said she could do nothing here for these tiny scraps of life.

Father O'Leary said he would fetch me next prison visiting day, I never went for I was laid low with a bad attack of Nigerian tummy ten times worse, I thought, than Kenyan tummy. I seemed unable to control either end, thankfully Jennie didn't go in for carpets.

Lydia was visiting and heard me, she cleaned up all round me, got me into bed, suitably supplied me with utensils and polished me up in a very short time. She had once, it seemed, trained as a nurse and I was more than grateful to her, I felt guilty too, that I didn't particularly like her but I had to admire her efficiency. I suppose it's possible to dislike and admire and be grateful to someone all at the same time.

Although no longer the 'White Mans Grave' Nigeria's climate and the conditions there did seem to favour a certain amount of illness. When the wind from the Sahara blew everyone seemed to have something, this North wind called the Harmattan brought a fine red dust that settled on everything. The diseases I called harmattanitis because it took so many forms, bad throats, rashes, sore eyes and bad tempers. Any minor ailment can be blamed on this wind but it was also accused of bringing in meningitis, whether this was true or not I never discovered. We washed the dust out of our hair and off our clothes and we dusted and dusted, eventually it died down. Elizabeth was endlessly dusted but she kept remarkably well.

Any washing that was dried outside had to be ironed because of the mango or 'butsi' fly. This lays its eggs on convenient damp clothes and if not killed by a hot iron the emerging grub burrows under the human skin and develops in a boil like lump. Jennie became quite proficient at removing these grubs from our friends. I only had two of these pests on my back from which Jennie removed a fat grub, after this I dried my underwear indoors just to be on the safe side.

Jennie had one of those baby carriers which holds the baby in the front, a neat navy blue affair very different from the bright cloth that attaches the baby to a large African behind.

"Excuse me, Madame," one of these ladies would say, stopping Jennie, "Babies are carried on the back." Jennie smiled sweetly.

"This one is carried in the front," she pointed out reasonably. The baby would be admired but always referred to as 'He'.

"Its a girl, she is wearing a frock."

"But," she was told, "He is not wearing earrings."

There are cultural differences even in the baby world.

Sometimes I took Elizabeth in her pram and walked her about the roads in the vicinity of the chicken farm and our bungalow. The rough red roads were not ideal for pram pushing but it gave me a good idea of the local terrain. I liked to tell myself that here I was in Wildest West Africa but I ever managed to convince myself, it was too suburban. I did feel one up on some of the adventuresses, none of them ever took a baby along, certainly not in a pram.

In the distance I could see a lake and I was determined to try and get near to it. There were no crocodiles and I eventually decided that it was the town's water supply, it was too swampy near the edge to attempt to push a pram.

I was fascinated by the building technique, the scaffolding, as in Kenya, was made of not very straight trees and it looked very rickety. I had a feeling that some of these houses were built on the save up and buy a block system, one would be added every two or three days. If you do it this way you do eventually own a house, it's one way of doing it.

While on one of my walks I came upon a good, finished but unoccupied house which had an unoccupied with water swimming pool. I stood and gazed at this desirable commodity and imagined the wonder of cool, clear water. What a terrible waste of what looked a good pool, why or why hadn't the project taken on this one.

There was a vast amount of pale blue paint everywhere, it was on houses, walls, stone and even trees. I wondered if it was supposed to bring an element of coolness to the place or if someone had bought vast quantities of the stuff and were selling it cheaply. It showed the dirt - the red dust that is always there.

We went with Simon when he attended a conference at the International Institute for Tropical Agriculture or IITA which is financed mainly with American money. It was an oasis in the middle of a red dusty, overcrowded and polluted African town. It seemed unreal when we first arrived and approached it by a green avenue of palm trees amid well kept grass and with a park containing other interesting trees.

Supper was American, there seemed to be no shortages such as we had been experiencing, it included beefburgers, waffles and baked beans. My room was cool and very quiet, the bed comfortable, I slept like a log.

Next morning after breakfast (more waffles and baked beans) and while Simon was in conference, Jennie and I wheeled the baby round the park and then spent the rest of the day by a crystal clear pool drinking ice cold cokes or lemonade and eating appetizing sandwiches. Being guests we had to pay for this so it was just as well that the visit was a short one.

I was amazed to hear that some of the scientists working there had never been outside the compound. One, working on the chick pea, had been there for three years. Did he, on returning to America, tell folks back home that he had spent this time in Nigeria?

The conference ended but I felt relief in returning to what, I had become to think of, as reality. I thought it pointless to live in this vacuum. It had no place in my idea of travel. I think oasis was the wrong word, cocoon would be a better one. It was enveloped against the noisy, colourful, bustling chaos that is the surrounding 'Africa'. I enjoyed the serene quiet break but was glad that Simon and Jennie preferred to be part of the life of the country as far as this was possible.

I am not trying to pretend that they lived what could be called 'going native'. There is a difference though between this and an insistence of transplanting your home sphere with your luggage as do so many expatriates. In so doing they miss out not only on knowledge but the gaining of many new friends.

I had a certain sympathy with the lets-not-notice-the-outside-world type because everything was so inefficient. It was a mystery to me that it should be so and even more of a mystery that I had begun to think of it as normal. The power would go off without warning at any time of the day or night. Telephones and the post were unreliable, hospitals and roads bad, accidents horrific, officials were rude and there were shortages of everything except plastics. I had thought that with its oil this was a rich country yet it seemed so poor. Was it mismanagement? This was no longer the West Africa of the early explorers, it had been conquered by the internal combustion engine, money was wasted on schemes that never prospered, it had had internal strife and was now struggling to cope with its growing millions. But this is my own story, I never meant it to be political or critical, however I saw and experienced all this and it surprised and saddened me. I was glad I was experiencing it and not cocooned in my own little world.

Simon had some days off and decided that we should go on a Safari. There was a game reserve called Borgu which he thought we should visit along with the Kainji reservoir and dam.

"Its all got a great write-up and there's plenty of wildlife in the reserve," enthused Simon waving a tatty dog-eared looking pamphlet but, while reassuring us on how good it was going to be, added, "Better be on the safe side and take everything with us." He was beginning to know Nigeria.

It was an interesting Safari, not from the animal point of view for we saw none of the more exciting mammals, but as a comparison with the tourist orientated Kenya.

In the game reserve we had to pick up a ranger, I suppose the object of his presence was to point out or protect the abundant wildlife, we saw none of any size and as he would not let us get out of the vehicle we couldn't say if there were any small creatures.

His name sounded like Silly and he proved worth his weight in gold as he was a dab hand with the tse-tse fly, many of which managed to get inside the vehicle. This was the most dangerous thing we saw, with visions of slides of trypanosome in my student days, it was good to see how proficient he was.

This was the emptiest part of Nigeria I had seen so far, not surprising if the tse-tse fly was abundant. Also I suppose animals disappear as the population grows, however we saw plenty of trees and plants and I enjoyed the drive.

There was a tiny uninteresting museum when we dropped off Silly, very different from the well stocked and profitable museums and gift shops in Kenya. I felt that the Nigerian authorities still had a long way to go in their attempts to create a tourist trade, so far it didn't seem very successful.

We then visited the Kainji reservoir and dam, this was very impressive and looked as if it worked, I saw fish eagles here, the first I'd seen, big and beautiful as they swooped into the water.

We were then ready for the 'Motel'. I have put inverted commas for here again there was little resemblance between this and what is generally recognized by the word. The dirt road was rough and the huts basic. A bed, a chair with a broken leg, a basin with one tap, lots of dead flies and no water. There was, luckily, a mosquito net as mosquitos buzzed around all night. We had taken heed of Simon's philosophical misgivings and brought all we needed including provisions as the 'dining hall' had little to offer, nothing was clean, the furniture was rickety, the crockery chipped.

There was a trader here trading in skins of various endangered species as well as the usual trinkets. We didn't buy anything.

Perhaps this 'motel' wasn't the one in the write-up. It hardly resembled the description, maybe it had deteriorated since then or perhaps it was still in a learning situation. When we met up with it it was definitely dilapidated. Not surprisingly we were the only guests and we enjoyed the quiet. We were still one up on the Victorian travellers for we had a roof and if the eggs they fried us for breakfast were a little greasy we were anything but starving. We all had our photographs taken and Madame said that should we ever wish to stay in the hotel we should be welcome, the rooms were good, she said. They were a good size but we preferred the huts as they did have doors. The dirty curtains that fulfilled the same purpose in the hotel left much to be desired. We all smiled, shook hands, and left.

Back at the bungalow the day of departure drew near and it was time to pack again, even the extension to my visa had nearly run out.

The day of departure is no ordinary event in Nigeria, presents arrive for Mother and, the post being what it is, mail for posting in the U.K. A large party gathered ostensibly to wish me Bon Voyage but in reality to make sure that I had all the letters safely especially as so many of them hadn't any stamps. I promised faithfully that all would be well. Jennie had promised me a Goodbye supper but she could not feed all these so it was nearly mid-night when we sat down to the charred remains of a hard won chicken. We didn't fancy it by then anyway.

It was an evening flight and we all went down to Lagos. Simon had a meeting there and had arranged it to fit in with my departure. Jennie was going to stay with friends, show off Elizabeth and stock up with items unobtainable further north.

I hadn't realized that I should find the 'goodbyes' so difficult as I tore myself away to join once more the African chaos with the pushing and shouting that made up the Airport battle. Somewhere out there, I hoped, was an aeroplane and once through the officialdom it was there. I watched again that strange transformation on the plane back to a dull, suited, quiet collection of people.

It really seemed cold back in England after the sweating heat of Lagos. A few snowflakes fell.

I now had a bad disease. I call it Africanitis and as I watched the snow I was already planning the next trip.

* * *

I am walking along a quiet sandy road and I can hear someone calling me from a long way off. It must be time for Elizabeth's bath or perhaps Simon and Jennie want to go out.

Suddenly I am awake.

"If you want to sleep," says Tom, "Why not do it in bed where I'm just going?"

To his surprise I burst into tears. They are so far away.

Tom is so upset he makes me a cup of cocoa even with the full knowledge that I am not a cocoa person.

"I thought it was Jennie," I explain, but I can see he is hurt so I down the cocoa wishing it was a double brandy.

I think of Freya Stark and her words about managing and doing without things.

There's next year and I shall be there.

CHAPTER 6

I was welcomed back at the prison, I hoped it was for myself and not only because the rest of the staff were booking summer holidays and felt that here was one who wouldn't be demanding the best weeks. But I had gained an aura. "She travels you know," or "she always goes somewhere exotic in the winter". This was more like it. Now that I knew what I wanted, all the saving, the managing, the doing without things, came easily. I enjoyed the job anyway and I now had a purpose for which I needed the money.

Simon, Jennie and Elizabeth came home for Christmas that year. I had worked hard all summer and I had also taken some private pupils, young people needing help with reading or assistance and encouragement with exams. I was ready for a break and after a wonderful Christmas when we were joined by Amanda, Michael, George and Victoria, I set out again for a visit to Paula and my now many friends in Kenya. I'd begged Paula to visit us but I soon realized that it was very unlikely that she would. The safaris she was tempting me with were too good to miss. Amboseli was still on the list of, as yet, unvisited regions.

Some of my journeys I can remember well, even small day to day happenings, some I find, I cannot remember at all.

At first I found that this one was one of those. My grotty bits of paper and strange notes meant nothing to me. What, for instance could Bogoria-hot-hippo-staring mean? Bogoria is a soda lake, and there cannot have been hippos there and was it staring or starving or merely looking at me in a bloodshot hungry way?

Perhaps my photographs could help, though I often forget my camera at a time when I really need it. Then as I rummaged through I found that this had been a bad storage year, some were stuck together and others looked as if they had been chewed by mice. However memory started to return as bits of paper and saved memorabilia tumbled out of my disorganized folders.

There is no mention of Amboseli and I am fairly sure we never got there.

Lake Bogoria I remember in all its spectacular beauty. I loved it, great black sheer cliffs standing up in the background of this exciting place. This is how a rift valley lake should look and, yes, it was hot. Hot, too, are the steaming boiling fountains and bubbling mud, it is almost frightening in its elemental beauty. I expected it to be dramatic and it was.

Added to this are the pink mass of flamingos, these only live on the soda lakes where a special algae thrives.

The wonder for me was the fact that I was there, no travel films can ever prepare you for the reality, to be there is the experience, I am me and I am here, I am a part of this amazing scenery.

But what about the Hippo? It must have been at Baringo for I have photographs of that lake too, there are no flamingos here but it is famous for other wildlife including the hippopotamus. This one insisted I was his best friend and could-he-come-in-please. I've heard that hippos can be dangerous and I didn't like to test it so I crept around the back of my hut to Paula's huge enjoyment. I still don't know if it was staring or starving but as there appeared to be plenty of vegetation about, it couldn't have been this, unless he was having dental problems.

"Perhaps he thought you were a dentist," suggested Paula when I put forward this theory.

We returned to Nairobi. I was no longer suffering from culture shock, the roads, the red soil, the endless walkers, all seemed familiar and normal. The Kenyans are great walkers, it is no surprise to me to see them winning Olympic medals.

I started to notice more things such as the overloaded buses and 'matatus' with passengers and their strange parcels hanging round every space, on the sides, the back and the roof. There were spot checks along the routes and to avoid trouble passengers were dropped off before a check-point and reloaded when all was clear, the trek around the back accepted as part of the journey. Was it a recognized routine or merely ignored? The police were doing their job in making sure that vehicles were not overloaded.

There are photographs too of the beach and Dorothy is with us. I shall never tire of these wonderful stretches of golden sand, the palm trees and the warm Indian Ocean. A friend of Dorothy's offered us a simple coast cottage and the three of us went down to this beautiful place again. It has a wonderful beach on which to get an enviable tan, an absolute necessity to show off to one's friends.

We were somewhat pestered this time by sellers on the beach, carvings and beads being the usual wares. Some of the hotel beaches have guards and the beach is safe but here we were on our own, one had to stay behind minding things while the others swam. We took it in turns.

A small group of men wandered up to us and Dorothy, in all innocence and, seeing they weren't carrying goods, asked one of them what he had to offer, she was taken aback when he started to undo his shorts to reveal his not insignificant masculine appendages.

I decided to return to within our own walls and we all removed ourselves to the cottage, its garden was sand anyway.

Perhaps it's unwise for women on their own to wander here but perhaps, too, there was custom for these hopeful young men. Who am I to put a damper on their enterprise?

I asked Paula what they charged.

"There you have me," she paused "But you'd get something out of it. Disease."

"My interest was merely academic," I replied. But for me the beach had lost its glamour and there was a cloud in the bright blue sky.

"Gordon has been asking about you," said Jeff, a friend of Paulas, "He's just come back from Nigeria. You'll have a lot to talk about. He didn't like it much," he added.

This was putting it mildly. Gordon couldn't say enough evil about the place. He'd bored everyone telling them how awful it was.

I spotted him one morning in Nairobi when I was sitting in an outdoor restaurant, he didn't look well. I think he wanted sympathy and I was willing to let him talk himself out. His manner did not endear him to people so that there was a general feeling that he had it coming to him. He'd ended up in a Nigerian gaol, mistaken identity as it turned out, but it had certainly soured him.

"What were you doing there in the first place?" I asked.

"I was working," he replied defensively. "They mistook me for someone else, I can't tell you how humiliating and degrading it was, I shall never, never, never go back there."

I have to admit to all the bad things that are said about Nigeria and I am sure their prisons are places to avoid but for me Nigeria has a richness only seen in West Africa. I grumble about the heat but lap up its warmth, I grumble about the hygiene but long for that unmistakable smell, I grumble often about the people but I love the genuine Nigerian before officialdom has spoiled him. I grumble about the noise or noises, for there are so many different ones, notably the strange sound of the crickets when the sun goes down. Then there are the bright cheerful drapes of the women often beautifully matching with wonderful colours. To see these women balancing great loads on their heads, effortlessly and with their graceful carriage, is a sight indeed.

So I cannot say 'never again', but I agree with him cheerfully.

"We must go for another trip again," he said brightly.

"Why not?" I replied but know it will never take place for I have every intention of returning to Nigeria.

I met Gordon again very briefly in London when I was 'doing' museums with George.

"I must tell mum," said George who had treated Gordon with great suspicion.

"Tell her what?" I asked in some alarm.

"About your boy friend," he answered reprovingly and with a knowing look.

I let it pass, though I nearly said, "Tell Tale."

My son's postcards are tantalizing. In a few words he tells me so much and so little.

"There are two airports here," he writes. "One is spacious, air-conditioned and with all facilities - I am at the other one."

Or, on the back of a postcard showing magnificent mountain scenery, "Where I am is not remotely like this, I am on a mud flat."

I look out of the window, the sky is black and it has poured for days. I am on a mud flat too.

Now I have a picture of two pink clad musical Nigerians. Why is the stamp on the wrong side?

"We have moved house, it is bigger with more garden. Can you bring a swimming pool when you come?"

How do you carry a swimming pool in your luggage?

I soon found out, they come in kit form with metal poles and a plastic lining, the completed pool stands upwards instead of downwards and has a side ladder. They looked very pretty in the folder pictures. I was still considering its transport when I had another card, this one depicted rolls of material on what looked like a local craft stall. The card was brief again.

"Don't bother with swimming pool, Jennie is coming home to have the baby. We can bring it back with us. Shall you come?"

I am left wondering if I am mistaken about what I think it says. Its the first I've heard about a baby and I hope they will be taking it back with them. I reply that, "Yes, I will come," and leave it at that.

* * *

I make the mistake of meeting Jennie at Heathrow in my mini instead of hiring a pantechnicon. How we squeezed everything in I shall never know. Jennie herself had expanded a good deal and Elizabeth had grown, added to this was her pram and the vast amount of paraphernalia associated with young children. She appeared to have lost a favourite toy called 'Hugger-dog' and was not going to be put off with any substitute. They were both cold as our English summer in no way compared with the heat of Nigeria. Then we had to unpack the mini to try and find Huggerdog while Elizabeth cried in gentle misery. It was nowhere to be found so we repacked and Elizabeth was almost smothered with luggage, fortunately too overwhelmed to cry and she soon fell asleep. We stopped in Reading on the way, found a toy shop and a new Huggerdog. We persuaded Elizabeth when she awoke that he had had a nice wash and brush up. She seemed satisfied.

Adam arrived before Simon could return. He looked exactly like his sister and was another flaming red-head.

"Why you no wait?" Simon telexed.

I returned with them in late Autumn, they had become acclimatized to English weather again and Lagos airport was very hot. Elizabeth had been in a deep sleep and was now fractious, Adam was crying because he wanted to. Now was the time to try out my theory which was based upon the Nigerians' fondness for children. Would the official rudeness and disregard for passengers, which is apparently essential for their dignity, give way to their natural caring and affection?

"Let me take Adam," I said firmly, Jennie was trying to cope with Elizabeth and the usual trappings, Simon was going through the documents to make sure he had all the necessary papers. It was a long queue and we were well back. No-one can stop a loving and weary grandma from wandering out of the queue and leaning against the official desks. Adam gave voice with the full power of his young lungs. He was hot, he was in a strange place and now an added trouble - he couldn't see his mother.

"Where your family?" asked the official.

I pointed to them well down the queue, he sent someone to bring them forward, even the passengers just going through looked relieved. Simon lost his look of weary tolerant acceptance. Over the years he had become resigned to the situation.

"Well done, Mother," he said cheerfully.

My theory was proved, compassion had won, the trouble is I am not always carrying a screaming baby.

We had a very pleasant and quiet night at the rest house and next morning a good shopping trip before travelling up North. I found Lagos even more confusing than before and I was glad when we drove up the north road and away from its noisy vastness.

I liked the new house, a proper house this time with a staircase. My room was downstairs and I had two bathrooms, excellent so long as there is water. The other bedrooms were upstairs and Lizzie, as she now wished to be called, had her own room.

Lydia was now our next door neighbour. Perhaps, I told myself, a good thing if I again had Nigerian tummy, a selfish outlook of which I was aware. She did so like to be in on everything and give everyone the benefit of her knowledge whether she had any or not.

There was a wall between the two houses and she came bustling towards me as I was admiring a great orange lizard sunning itself upon it.

"They're poisonous, you know," she warned with a smile of anticipation of my horror.

"I wasn't thinking of eating them," I retorted. I meant to snub but not to snub too hard for she was a dead cert if my need came again and I was ill. She was slightly possessive of me now for I was one of her patients. I tried to be a grateful one.

The geologist had arrived, I was delighted by this as I felt slightly responsible for his appointment. Now, many years later, I can look back and say 'thank goodness' as he Ben, and his wife Alison, have remained firm friends. Ben, gentle, knowledgeable and friendly, I was a little in love with him but I could extend this to Alison, life here was better for having them. They were not new to Africa and Alison had always travelled with Ben and lived in all sorts of conditions.

Ben came over as soon as we arrived to pay his respects to Simon's Mother.

"Alison isn't well," he said, "I don't know what's the matter."

"Shall I come over?" asked Jennie.

"Would you?" asked Ben hopefully.

"Is it harmattanitis?" I now put in the suggestion.

Ben brightened and smiled.

"An excellent term," he said. He departed more cheerfully.

Jennie was galvanized into action, we made some cakes and went visiting at tea-time.

"You'll like Alison," said Jennie. I find this off-putting but I was prepared to if Jennie and she had struck up a friendship. I think the cheering up worked, I think she had been missing Jennie and had so much looked forward to her return and the coming of Adam.

Harmattanitis takes all forms and has no particular symptoms. Reassurance that one hasn't got leprosy or cancer or some other dread disease is often all that is needed.

The swimming pool arrived shortly after this, we hadn't travelled with it in our laps. Everybody collected to see it sited, constructed and eventually filled.

A party was suggested but Simon, who loves building bits onto things, seemed to think that a house extension in the form of a verandah was necessary, it was to be both protection from rain or sun. I could visualize this "bit of a verandah" but my idea bore no relation to the eventual gracious and ample area that served for bathing parties. One of Simon's friends was in the building trade, he was a large happy Italian called Luigi and bringing friends and men with equally expansive ideas created this beautiful addition. A few hangers on and their relations had helped, glad of a little extra cash, and the whole was up in a very short time, no planning permission was needed and the landlord would be delighted.

"I wish there was a garden centre," I said to Jennie as we drew back to admire their handiwork.

"All it wants is some plants," she agreed.

"There is a garden centre," said Luigi, "Of sorts," he added. He went on to explain to Jennie just where it was.

It took us a very short time to tuck Adam under one arm - he had been longing to get into the wet cement for some time - get into the car and be on our way.

Perhaps by Nigerian standards it was a garden centre. Certainly there were plants and we bought some of the best from a disinterested gardener/salesman. I'm not sure which he was, as a gardener he should have been looking after and watering the rows and rows of neglected plants, as a salesman he should have been trying to sell them. Neither of us were very knowledgeable on Nigerian plants.

"I want one of those orange things," said Jennie, unbotanically. Bougainvillaea we did know and we included some of these in our varied and uncertain collection.

These were planted before nightfall and, being Nigeria, looked by the end of the week as if they'd been there for years almost hiding the fine Italian pillars.

We were all ready for a swimming party.

It was in full swing when we realized that a large number of people, mostly children, had gathered and we had an appreciative audience. Simon was galvanized next day into preventing this local amusement.

"You are a spoil sport," I accused him, "They were having a lovely time viewing the strangers' water sports in their even stranger contraption."

"They can go and have a lovely time looking at someone else," he retorted as he unloaded and started to fix up some fancy grass fence.

When Simon started something it was down tools, be it spade or broom, for any of the men. The boss was always such a pleasant distraction and they never knew what he would be up to next. The fence was hand woven and, although we could no longer see the onlookers, it didn't prevent peepholes appearing in it at all levels. So everyone had their fun.

Christmas approached and hunts for food, presents and decorations started. Back home this starts in October but here we didn't get into the atmosphere until a few days before. Perhaps it was the lack of snow, it was very hot. We had a big party and everyone contributed something and if it was only chick peas instead of sprouts no-one seemed to mind.

Ben had been persuaded to be Father Christmas, he was as nervous as a first night actor and it was not the best costume for the weather but no child said "Why, it's only Ben," so it was a successful role. The locals gathered to see this quaint custom, obviously some sort of medicine man or witch doctor, and what was in that mysterious sack? What spells would he cast?

One morning at breakfast I saw my son-in-law Michael at the gate. Everyone had tried to prevent him from leaving the safety of his Lagos hotel to visit in the unknown interior! He insisted that if his Mother-in-law could, he could.

"You go on about the early travellers," he said, "But they made it sound just like the first dangerous explorations."

And I'd thought it was all rather tame. I knew Michael did business in Nigeria but I had not expected to see him. We had a party on the strength of his visit.

'Rather tame' I have just written but also cosy and very domestic, perhaps in our new location almost suburban.

Perhaps it was more exciting for those early explorers but all travel and interest in new surroundings is only insight into other people's domesticity. I except those travellers for whom wild vast expanses of desert are a necessity. For me sand and sand and more sand becomes a trifle boring. I have seen it from the air and find it daunting and somewhat frightening, perhaps that is its appeal.

So my book is shamelessly domestic. I have not studied anything seriously and, apart from a few paintings and some rather poor quality photographs, have little record of my wanderings. There is this book of course.

CHAPTER 7

One morning I was up early, it was cooler in the dawn and I was savouring that first cup of tea.

Simon joined me, "Do you want to come with me to visit the farmers," he asked.

Did I? This was just what I did want and had been hoping for. I wanted to see the villages and the people there. Domestic still, but someone else's.

It was just as I imagined it for we were there among the people not just driving through on an uninteresting main road, detached from reality.

The villagers turned out, the children clamoured and followed me everywhere, I was a novelty and everyone was so curious and so kind. "Mama, mama," they called. Had it changed all that much over the years? Sadly I came in a Land Rover and not with a hundred bearers.

Simon, welcomed and no longer a stranger, was amused by the excitement I caused.

There was poverty here but I didn't see any serious malnutrition and nothing like the shanty towns in Lagos or Nairobi.

"If they ask you advice or bring their illnesses to you tell them a government health visitor is on the way. They may not understand you anyway," said Simon.

They probably didn't and I wasn't carrying so much as an aspirin.

Simon seemed to be able to communicate nodding and smiling cheerfully while getting his message over. There was always someone in the village who understood and spoke English and there was always the driver if all else failed.

The Headman was the most likely to have some English or Pidgin. Pidgin is a language in its own right and is easily translatable. The Headman could be recognized by his air of authority, his better clothes and, as a badge of office his fly-whisk, a short grass switch with a beautifully decorated bead handle.

Fortunately nobody brought me any dread diseases to heal.

Jennie lent me a wonderful book entitled "Where there is no Doctor".

"You never know," she said.

"Read the chapter on Black Magic and how to combat it," she added.

I'd been told that some of this was still practised and I've no doubt that I was viewed as some very odd white witch.

I loved Jennie's book, it was full of common sense, cleanliness is stressed, not always so easy in a drought and if the well dries up. There were several horrifying pictures by the author, I was lucky never to be confronted with bullet wounds, broken limbs or leprosy, nor was I asked to deliver a baby. I was thankful for this, the huts looked dark and it was better to socialize outside. Not only that, my midwifery was practically non-existent.

I learnt to carry aspirin and sweets for the children, I felt guilty about the sweets as the children had such wondrous white and gleaming smiles, was I spoiling those teeth? The aspirin wouldn't do any harm and might alleviate pain until a government health official arrived.

I always took my camera, everyone wanted to be photographed and I was taken triumphantly to see the harvest. Who needs words when you can stand by stacks of food. "Take me by all these lovely bags bursting with crops" is obvious in any language.

I grew to value these visits with Simon. He liked someone to talk to as we drove around and the driver though cheerful and helpful was not a great conversationalist. I asked so many questions when I didn't recognize a plant, I saw things growing I had never expected to see. I'd always hated tapioca pudding and felt justified in my dislike when I saw this gross, swollen root. It bore no resemblance to that final product. The plant is called Cassava or Manioc, all sorts of other things can be done with it, there's a meal called Garri, and I believe an alcoholic drink. Its a shrubby plant with leaves a bit like a horse chestnut and is a useful starchy food. Simon wasn't interested in it, for one thing I'd never fed tapioca pudding to my own children and another, he was trying to introduce more protein into the local diet. This means more peas and beans and intercropping them. There was also the soya bean, but more of this later.

I'd heard and seen the yam pounding, I now saw this growing in great mounds of earth. This isn't a book about tropical agriculture, although growing things is part of village life and most people's lives revolved around the basics of life such as eating and drinking. These small farms were something like the Kenyan 'shambas'.

"They're not all small farmers," Simon told me, "Some have more than one plot and are considered quite rich."

We went out of our way to visit a vast sugar growing area with a big factory for its manufacture. I was told that there were many snakes hidden in the canes so I didn't venture into the thick growth. My greatest treat was to see the cocoa bean growing, my father having worked for a well known chocolate firm and had refused to visit 'the white man's grave' - Nigeria.

Simon had this 'thing' about the soya bean and brought a sack of the seeds and put them in one of the downstairs baths - luckily it had a door. I don't remember the object of the experiment but I shall never forget the smell. Perhaps he meant to germinate them there and plant them, (I hope elsewhere) but they rotted and the stink permeated the whole house. I have never eaten Soya in any form since although I probably wouldn't recognize it in ice cream. Alison made a pink pudding of some derivative, as she was serving it out it stuck to the spoon, she gave an extra shake, it bounced from the plate to the ceiling. It was a hilarious dinner party. I still don't remember if we ate it. I think this was in the early days of soya bean. Perhaps Simon's experiments were in the nature of an alcoholic breakthrough.

Our domestic peace was disturbed when the Nigerians decided to throw out the Ghanaians. Sammy was a Ghanaian, and the Nigerians were about with guns. It was all very well for Alison to say "Don't point that thing at me, young man," with the firm belief that it was not loaded. A Ghanaian couldn't be so sure. After all, some time back they had thrown out the Nigerians. Tit for Tat.

Sammy came in tears, "Many men with guns, we want to go."

I hadn't had a chance to spend any money, there was so little to spend it on and I had changed some only the week before. Perhaps I am a sucker for a hard luck tale but I told Sammy he could hire the bus he needed, collect his friends and return to the safety of his own country.

Simon wasn't too pleased, "I told him he could go, I'm not stopping him. Your money will all go on drink!

He was wrong.

A loaded vehicle, more an old truck than a bus, arrived at the gate, loaded is an understatement, it was crowded with people and hung about with their goods. They had come to say "Thankyou and Goodbye."

I was as surprised as Simon and, as we waved them off, I feel fairly sure Simon had his hand in his pocket just before shaking hands with Sammy, these things are best ignored, a handshake can conceal much.

I knew no names or addresses, I remembered this after I had accepted all the invitations to visit Ghana, I haven't been there - yet. I had the satisfaction of knowing that some at least hadn't been bullied or merely shot.

My time too was running out and I had many goodbyes to say on my own account. I knew more about the villages now and of the villagers need for a good gossip around the water tap. I had learnt how to tell a village with better community spirit by its latrine. Of course I was an excitement, I was as good as the telly and I was no longer embarrassed by the sensation I caused.

I had one new acquaintance to make. I'd heard about Denise, Jennie and I had met her husband in the town and he said she was away in Paris. Lydia shook her head mournfully when she heard Denise was returning and somehow managed to convey the impression that this was not the sort of person whose company I should enjoy. She even made a stay in Paris sound disreputable.

"Just wait and see, don't go by what Lydia says," said Alison laughing. Jennie agreed.

Perhaps it was the Paris bit that made me think she was French so I was totally unprepared for a North country delightful personality. She wasn't beautiful, perhaps dynamic is the word, she delighted me from the first meeting, poor Lydia, no wonder she couldn't blossom in this presence. Denise had been longing to meet Adam, she came straight to him, it was love at first sight for both of them, she could hardly bear to part from him. I often wondered what was the attraction between this skinny blond with the laughing brown eyes and the fat little red-head.

My family 'goodbyes' were to be at the airport.

We'll have a few days down there," said Simon, "You'll like Bar beach, there are simple beach shelters there and you can visit those stalls for presents."

There were no stalls, they were run by Ghanians and had been destroyed by the Nigerians. There was nothing there. Why does man have to be so destructive? I hope the stall-holders and their goods found a bus to get themselves away. Perhaps I should find those batiks I fancied if ever I visited Ghana.

We stayed at the resthouse and saw something of this extraordinary strange and varied coastline, the river Niger forming a great delta here. Mary Kingsley describes it as a river "much given to going into lagoons and mud". I like this description but I think a good deal of dredging has been done since her day. There is now a great harbour here, it's a big modern port. There are still islands, creeks and lagoons, I'd love to explore here in a small boat with a reliable boatman. Further west beyond Bar beach, where we were going, the coastline continues in a network of creeks and here are the mangrove trees with their curious gnarled roots half out of the water.

Simon and Jennie had been to Bar beach before, they described it as the perfect tropical beach, lovely sand with a backing of palm trees, simple thatch shelters and plenty of room in the palm grove for a barbecue. It was every bit as good as they described it. On the days we were there the waves were breaking on the shore with greater force than I'd expected, it was beautifully refreshing, but, as far as I was concerned, not a swimming sea.

The barbecue was lit and as I sat outside a hut where Adam was peacefully sleeping, Simon brought me a coconut still in its husk, a man had climbed a palm and brought it down for him. A hole was made in it, a straw and rum added, "Try this," said Simon. I can't describe this superb drink. Back home I've tried to reproduce it but failed miserably, perhaps it needs a coconut straight from the tree or perhaps the warm sun and sand.

Some friends of Simon and Jennie joined us on the beach. I sat watching them playing on the sea edge, I didn't join them, my excuse being that I was minding Adam but I doubted my ability to stand. I am not given to daytime drinking, it was a superb day so relaxed and with a sense of wellbeing I joined the sleeping Adam in the hut.

These few days were a wonderful end to my visit.

I left from Lagos Airport.

I am home again and I try not to fall asleep and dream I am still there. As Tom so reasonably puts it, "I'd thought you'd be glad to be home, you've got everything you want and it all works including the television."

Everything I want. Yes, I do have everything material that I need. I can pick up a telephone and phone Amanda or any of my friends. I can switch on television and enjoy and choice of programmes for there will be a choice. I have a car and I can go shopping in shops with well stocked shelves. I can go out for a meal and not expect food poisoning. I can switch on the lights and lighten the darkness. How can I explain to Tom when I can see how hurt he is? I can see the old cocoa coming up and it comes to me that I have now seen the cocoa bean growing. I am greatly cheered by this thought and, yes, I can see it again next year.

I returned once more to Nigeria. Ben and Alison had been on leave and we were travelling back together. It was while waiting for them at the airport that I witnessed an incident of cultural difference. A large overweight rich looking Nigerian family were trying to bribe their way through the check desk. The luggage of this party was so overweight that they were being asked to pay £1,000 for excess baggage. Bribery was a way of life in Nigeria, and may be still for all I know, but over here you can do it by charm or a hard luck tale, never by bribery. The sad thing was that the Nigerian party did not recognize the fact and kept adding to the bribe pile while more officials gathered in tight-lipped disapproval.

I know about bribery in Nigeria but tried not to be involved.

And Mother Came Too   71

Some said, "You can't get on without it," others,"You can get anything that way," I also heard, "It helps to oil the wheels."

It must have been an example of oil-wheeling that I was witnessing at Gatwick. I never knew the outcome as Ben ad Alison arrived, we all went to another desk and my peculiar, odd shaped and definitely overweight luggage was passed through without question.

There was no trouble at the other end either as Ben, in his quiet way, in almost hushed tones explained it all away as necessary for "The Green Revolution".

A driver awaited the project geologist and we drove up North again.

There was no improvement in the road accidents.

"Bad, bad one here," said our driver and he was right. This was the worst I'd seen because it involved a great cattle truck and these poor creatures lay dead or dying all over the road. So many accidents with heavy trucks occur when two vehicles meet where the road narrows to bridge an often dry watercourse. Neither driver will give way, one loses and ends up upside down in the treacherous gully. Sometimes both lose.

Now there was nothing we could do, the only bright side was seeing villagers beginning to collect with unsympathetic and hungry eyes. There would be many full stomachs for some weeks to come. Ben remarked sadly that sometimes he wished he were a vet. Even a vet would have felt useless here.

The family were waiting at the gate as we arrived. An arrival is an excitement and had been anticipated with hopeful expectation. My luggage would be treasure trove. Elizabeth was now a self possessed young lady of 'nearly four' and Adam had grown from a fat little baby into a fat little toddler, he'd lost some of his flesh, but none of his charm. If roused he still had a powerful voice, he was shy at first but Lizzie, as she now liked to be called, was longing to show me round and tell me all the latest gossip.

"Where's the pool?" I asked immediately and anxiously as I could not see it in its accustomed place.

"Round the back," replied Simon firmly. He had tired of providing all the local entertainment, now it was hidden by one piece of screening. There must have been entertainment enough when the pool was moved with the water siphoned off into every local vessel, queues for the free supply, and no drop wasted, I am sorry I missed the fun.

There were new next door neighbours. Neil was living there with his new wife, Trudi. Lydia and Roy had returned to England, I wasn't sorry to see the back of their children. Last time I had been here I'd spotted another endearing trick that of pelting Elizabeth and Adam with bad tomatoes over the garden wall when they thought no-one was looking.

We saw little of Trudi who was Swiss and very domesticated, she occasionally visited with various embroidered or crocheted gifts. At the time I did not think of myself as a crochet receiver but I have it still as a reminder of the solid unruffled home loving Trudi. I can't think what she was doing in Nigeria, I could imagine her in a neat, clean Swiss chalet. She was a pleasant quiet neighbour making an occasion of any visit or presentation. Neil now seemed a better adjusted person so perhaps he was now up to happy practices of his own.

There were other new faces in our small society, a young newly married Kenyan couple called Alan and Hazel Martin were living in a caravan within a compound. We found we had mutual friends in Kenya and I was able to commiserate with them in their comparisons between the two countries.

There were domestic changes as well, our Sammy had gone, of course, and they missed his cheerful ways, the gardener had been moved inside.

"Is he any good at housework?" I now asked.

"Probably not," replied Simon, "But we knew him, he's honest and he likes it here." His perseverance had won the day.

Jennie had decided, wisely perhaps, to do the cooking and had a girl, Clara, to help in the kitchen. Clara had lost her own baby and last year had enjoyed tying Adam on to her ample behind African fashion. The children loved her and she was now promoted from the washing girl to inside girl, she was expecting again but only giggled when we asked about the father. Perhaps one of the two 'brothers' for the other one was to promoted to official gardener, he had always been there, the difference was he was now paid on a regular basis.

All was peace on the domestic front.

Christmas approached and we began to think of Christmassy things and persuading Ben to take up his duties as Father Christmas again. Then the Southalls arrived, Melanie and her two children Jacqueline and Steven. She had gathered them up from school on the last day of term and flown straight out to join Philip, they were still in school uniform and very confused. Jumpers and ties not being suitable for the weather. We hoped they would soon shed these but Melanie's ideas of luggage were very practical. She had been out before and now had a complete gastronomic Christmas dinner party in her various cases. Remembering last year's scrawny chicken we viewed the plump turkey with unbelieving eyes. Most people hadn't seen anything like this feast for months.

"I haven't forgotten the sprouts," she said while we gawped, "Who needs clothes in this climate," she continued defensively as the children sweated.

We stopped worrying about Christmas, Melanie had it all in hand, and all went well, of course. Ben again delighted the children and the usual crown gathered at the gate to watch the strange ceremony.

In the new year Simon heard of two British V.S.O girls in a remote village "somewhere north of us". The British Resident was away and had asked Simon to "keep an eye on things." Simon took this seriously when he heard through the grape-vine, the beating of drums or just plain rumour about these girls, it seemed a duty just up his street! He was encouraged by all the single young men on the various projects, not many had wanted to bring out their own girls.

"Let's go and look for them," said Simon. Jennie was busy, Adam stayed with her so with an interested Elizabeth and plenty of provisions we set out.

We found the village with some difficulty. People shook their heads when asked.

"Perhaps you're not pronouncing it correctly." I suggested unkindly as Lizzie started to get restless and I to get hungry.

"It must be somewhere around here," said Simon. "Let's ask at the nearest school, someone will know."

The proved to be an excellent idea, the only problem being that the teacher there wanted us to stay and perhaps talk to the children.

Lizzie was an immediate attraction.

We found the village and could see the school as we descended into a valley. Our arrival was an event and everyone came out to meet us. It was evident that no-one had seen a vehicle or any other Europeans for some time. The crowd around us included Margaret and Sally, the two British girls we had come to see. A holiday atmosphere prevailed. Lizzie was beginning to accept the attention she had as her due.

Margaret and Sally were both graduates and obviously had a spirit of adventure as well as being public spirited. A mathematics degree was of little use to children barely able to count and an English degree hardly helped with children unable to speak that language. The classes were huge and there were no educational facilities. It had been a shock. They had no transport and their 'house' certainly existed but it was a wooden shack with no furniture. A school holiday was declared, the young Nigerian 'head teacher' joining in the fun.

We were glad we had found them, they would have no lack of transport now, every young man on the projects would be on his way and gifts would include wonderful practical things such as a chair, a rag or a Calor gas light. A party was arranged for the weekend and we met them again there enjoying the interest they had caused. The Southalls had to return to England. We missed them, once the children recovered from their initial shock they were cheerful and played happily with our much younger couple. They considered the swimming pool adequate recompense for the magnificent Christmas spread.

Alison dropped in one morning suggesting we should all go shopping. Lizzie decided to stay with Clara and ride "me birthday bike," a dangerous, local made gaudy affair that Simon had found in the market - Lizzie loved it, Jennie, Adam and I went with Alison and in the middle of the hot, dusty, hooting and unrelenting traffic the car stopped and refused to go on. It was not only hot and dusty, it was almost unbreathably hot and dusty. Now was the time for Adam to give voice and rouse the town. How unpredictable children are, for now he bounced and gurgled smiled and waved his fat little hands at all and sundry. It might have been a treat put on especially for him. He attracted the attention of an old Muslim shop-keeper, an Alhaji according to his sign, who, seeing our predicament came out and offered shelter and refreshment within the cool of his shop. I accepted and Adam and I enjoyed his hospitality while Jennie and Alison fiddled uselessly with the car. Fortunately Ben came by before we had outstayed our welcome, Adam was still being charming as we left. I think now of this man's kindness and the uncaring crowd.

This was not our only car adventure, this time in Ibadan where Simon and Ben had another conference. We had left the children playing at the house of friends and were trying to find a craft centre. While concentrating on directions we went the wrong way round a roundabout and were chased, with siren blazing, by a police car. I know now what it is like to be in a chase and how the instinct is to put the foot down and hope to shake off your pursuer. We failed to do this and an enormous, angry and very drunk policeman proceeded to arrest us. He didn't, I am glad to say, handcuff us and put us in gaol but took us to some sort of club, even Jennie's placatory tones failed to soothe him. We were told not to leave, luckily there was a bar but we thought it safer to stick to soft drinks. Eventually a high ranking army officer arrived, we don't know who had contacted him, possibly the club manager. This officer then arrested the policeman for being drunk and we were free to go.

We were back home again when there was a 'coup'. The army was involved in this, they had taken over the government of the country with the intention of removing the corrupt regime. All seemed quiet and the streets were empty, perhaps the Nigerians were more used to 'coups' than I was.

Simon went into the town to enquire about things. He came back rather jollier than when he went, he sat down rather heavily, said "We've some leave due, we'll go tomorrow" and promptly fell asleep.

"I wonder who he has been seeing," I said to Jennie, thinking how official business must have tired him out.

"The local lads in a beer shop?" suggested Jennie as she, philosophical as always, proceeded to pack. I did the same, I'd no doubt that when he awoke it would be "Lets get this show on the road."

"I suppose there is a flight," I said dubiously, the seat of any trouble would most likely be in Lagos.

"If there isn't we can all go on the beach again," Simon replied cheerfully.

Some of our friends were staying, some decided to join our convoy.

"We'll put Mother in the front," said Simon, "No-one will shoot her."

If there's one thing I really appreciate in my son, it's his optimism.

There was a flight, most of us were able to get on it and I believe the rest of the party followed soon after. I am not fond of camping out in Airports.

The family returned six weeks later when all was quiet. Simon's contract finished in the Autumn, he decided then to study for a higher degree and was at University until the Summer. So far none of us have returned to Nigeria.

CHAPTER 8

The phone rang.

"Can you do some baby sitting?" asked Simon.

Normally my answer would be "Yes, of course," but they were living on the other side of the country, almost a day's journey and too far away to contemplate the usual evening sit-in. So my reply was guarded and thinking that perhaps a weekend invitation was coming up I said "Tell me more," with a tone of interrogation and hope.

"We're going to Norway, I thought you might like to come. Jennie and I are going on a Bemba course."

"A what course?" I asked disbelievingly and thinking it was some sort of unarmed combat or defence.

"Bemba," he repeated, "Its a tribal, language!" Nonchalantly he adds, "I've got a job in Zambia and by the way, Jennie is pregnant."

My mind races, I agree hastily to Norway, somehow I shall manage it, a nervous breakdown perhaps, and I ring off in order to have a quiet thinking session.

Where exactly is Zambia and how far pregnant is Jennie, being subjects worthy of a little meditation.

Zambia - surely this was the name of the old Northern Rhodesia? Isn't the Zambesi somewhere there? I was in the schoolroom again, luckily I had invested in a more up to date Atlas.

Jennie? How far pregnant was Jennie? I hadn't seen them for some time and this was the first I'd heard of it.

When we managed to meet up in London for a mammoth shopping-for-Zambia spree the event seemed imminent. George accompanied me on this trip, he doesn't like to be left out of an opportunity to spend other people's money. He was staying, anyway, and this was combined with educationally useful museum visit. A budding archaeologist, he wished to see some treasures taken from a recently discovered ancient wreck. He was a great 'help' with the shopping encouraging Jennie to "have the best one" after she'd had a year living on a student grant. He'd have liked to come to Norway with us but the small end-of-its-life / shabby student car could hardly squeeze in another passenger.

We drove to Norway in it.

When they met me I had great doubts about my ability to get in. I underestimated Simon who removed everything except Jennie who needed room and was sitting in the front seat. He then repacked everything around us declaring firmly that he knew where everything was. This repacking was to become typical of the journey, the roof and foot were full of camping things and there were bits and pieces all round us. Simon objected to my small bed but it went on the roof with the rest. I had translated "Don't bring any luggage" into "Bring only what you need" and I decided I needed my small camping bed. I admitted to my sleeping bag, a change of clothes (two as it happened) and something to wear in the evening. It was fairly tidy in the car at first but increasing chaos arose as hunts were made for some essential item such as tissues, drinks, sweets, a tape or a map.

There were three ferries on this journey which started at Harwich, we sailed to Esbjerg in Denmark, it was an all night crossing and I had a pleasant cabin, I was up early and found Simon and Liz already in a cafe, we spent a good deal of our time here but I did think Simon was adding to our luggage problem after a few visits to the duty free shop.

At Epsberg we drove a short way to a camping site and proceeded to put up our tent. It was a very shabby Boy Scout looking contraption and compared miserably with the beautiful cottage looking residences complete with furniture belonging to the Danish campers. We tried to look as if we were doing it this way because we were rugged eccentric British and not because we were stony broke so we used as much aplomb as we could in the whole proceeding of making ourselves at home. Simon is good at this. It was a beautiful site with showers and a shop. We tried to feel superior but were completely won over by the kindness of these people anxious to help us. We certainly looked as if we needed it. After some English practice on their side in which we were willing to help, we decided to retire and squeezed into the tent for the night, the others like sardines and I sideways at the door end, my bed now being an advantage as Simon's feet fitted underneath it.

Next day we drove across Denmark, there was one short ferry of an hour and another night crossing from Copenhagen. We loved Copenhagen, it is so tidy and neat, we had time for a quick look round and an excellent fish meal on the quay before joining our boat.

We disembarked at Oslo and after a preliminary look about the town we drove to the campus. Here we had a pleasant flat and soon settled in, we found the shop, the launderette and a children's playground, we could feed ourselves or visit the students' dining room. My baby sitting duties were not arduous, while Jennie and Simon were at classes we found all sorts of things to do and the shop sold "the best iced lollies in the world," according to Liz. There was a nearby lake and although too cold for me the children stripped off happily and splashed along with the hardy Norwegian children. We went to Oslo on the train and found a magnificent swimming pool, I could hardly say I was overworked.

When Simon and Jennie were free we were able to go further afield, the Norwegians expect and accept an apparent tough outlook, they themselves are geared to a weekend of outdoor life and our simple wilderness camping was appreciated here, no eyebrows were raised when we set out to explore with only bare essentials.

Our behaviour brought us to the notice of an attractive young man called Thor.

One supper time he said, "Why don't you come and visit us at the farm, please bring Mother too."

As he would be a neighbour in Zambia Simon cheerfully agreed to this invitation.

"Is it true," Thor asked, "That you had two babies in Nigeria and Mother went there?" he sounded disbelieving.

He didn't add that it looked as if another baby was also going out to Zambia.

We had a wonderful weekend there and met Thor's wife, Christina (or the Norwegian equivalent) and his two children. Christina's English was good and she was anxious to meet us. She was more than apprehensive about living in Africa and taking the children. The information and instructions she had received had served to frighten rather than reassure her. Thor wanted to introduce to her a family who not only took it all in their stride but also took out a new born babe and Mother. Christina showed us the advice she had received, this included do's and don'ts such as 'never go out in the sun' and 'cover up completely in the evening'. Added to this was information about injections to have before leaving, drugs to take with you and what to do about snake bite.

I began to think we should worry more as I read down lists of possible diseases. Yellow fever and malaria were the only two I took precautions against. What of cholera, amoebic dysentery, giardia or bilharzia? I preferred Jennie's book, we even had the Evil eye in that, not to mention the Butsi fly and leprosy. We kept quiet about these.

Simon and Jennie looked cheerful enough, Jennie said "the children have had more coughs and colds and minor upsets in the past year at home than they ever had in Nigeria."

"They also had chicken-pox." Simon reminded her, "And how many snakes did we see in Nigeria?"

Christina began to lose that worried look so we all cheered up and enjoyed their lavish hospitality. It was a lovely farm but in the snowbound winter half of the house was closed up while the family lived in a reduced and easier to warm central part. The Norwegians are more geared to the winter than we are in England, snow always takes us by surprise but in Norway it is expected and catered for. Skiing is a favourite sport there and even in summer Norwegians may be seen flexing their skiing muscles. We visited the Holmenkollen Ski Jump, this probably looks worse in summer but even in winter and covered in snow it must still appear daunting.

We made other friends who would also be going out to Zambia. One who wasn't was the attractive Bemba girl teacher, I had been reading all I could lay hands on about the Bemba people and one writer stated that they were the worst of the African tribes, lazy, untrustworthy and savage. If this girl teacher was typical of the tribe I think the writer got it wrong. After having living among them I am now sure of it, I found them delightful.

In the class with Simon and Jennie were a young newly-married English couple, Harry and Maureen. Later in Zambia I grew to appreciate Harry, always bouncing around, hopefully on the lookout for the latest gossip, he was the bush telegraph and was as reliable as the delivery of the morning paper.

We now tried to cram in as much as we possibly could and I am talking of our sightseeing and camping expeditions not of our stowing ability in the even more dilapidated vehicle. This procedure was generally watched by our friends in some wonder. We were not alone in our weekend devotion to the great outdoors, there was one drawback to this mass exodus from the towns, some touristy places closed down for all wanted to be away in the fine weather. This was some years ago and may have changed now as the tourist industry grows.

Our weekend camping took us to some beautiful spots by flowing streams and in unspoilt country, it seemed so quiet and empty seeing that so many appeared to have left the towns. It was idyllic.

Time went all too quickly and I had to return to work, I knew I had to go back to Norway sometime, I loved it so much and there was so much to see. With two small children activities had been restricted but we had visited the KonTiki raft and a Viking boat but then ice creams, a cafe or swimming seemed a necessity, or should I say the easy way out?

I decided to fly home and give the family more room in the car, they would then stay on another week as Thor had invited them to the farm again. The Norwegians were by then beginning to give Jennie funny looks as if they suspected her of being there for the Social Security. Jennie, on the other hand, was beginning to be anxious to be home, to have a British baby and not a Norwegian one which might have brought future difficulties. Neither did she fancy being caught out in the wilds or on a boat, she felt the time had come to return.

We had a farewell barbecue by the lake, I was glad it wasn't 'Goodbye'.

"See you at Christmas" everyone said. I had been back at work for three weeks when Simon rang.

"Another boy," he said. "We're calling him Peter."

Peter was a month old when they finally packed up, vacated their University flat and set off for Zambia.

CHAPTER 9

As Christmas approached I began to think once more of Africa, of winter in the sun, the journey and the amount in the cash box.

It came as a shock when Simon telexed "Don't come, writing!"

Now 'don't come' has much the same effect on me as 'come immediately'. I think of all the things that could have gone wrong and that they are trying to keep from me. I tell myself I must be brave and I must go out quickly in order to witness the tragedy for myself and to console the survivors. So I was already packing and had a flight booked when the letter arrived. "Have new house in view, alright for you to visit."

What then had happened to the old one? Had it been burnt down or been reduced to rubble in some way, an earthquake perhaps?

All became clear when a missing intermediate message arrived through Simon's firm, someone had been asked to send it and here it was, late but welcome.

"The house is tiny, hardly room for us, you would be sleeping with the computer." What's wrong with sleeping with a computer? I've slept with worse. I continued to pack.

The journey was uneventful and Simon met me at the airport. The arrival, although chaotic, was not as bad as Lagos. Somehow Simon was allowed through the barrier to help me with my luggage, a procedure not generally adopted at airports.

"We're staying tonight with friends called John and Lorna Harvey, they have a farm at a place called Chisamba, it's on our way," said Simon. "I think," he added.

"Oh," I said, "Can we find it?"

"I expect so," said Simon, "Lorna explained it. You'll like them."

Here I am in an unknown country for the first time and I've no idea where I am or how to get to some unknown people that I'm visiting. Its familiar, I relax.

If I'd known what I now know I shouldn't perhaps have been so happy. John and Lorna Harvey were so kind and helpful. Simon went out on an evening bird safari with John who was starting these and interested in developing tourism. They owned two more locations, one fantastic house at Shiwa Ngandu and another camp site where there were hot springs. Both of these we visited on other occasions.

The tragedy that happened took place here at Chisamba. I heard through the grapevine that John and Lorna had been shot, by whom I do not know or whether these criminals were ever brought to justice. Why kill such good people who had lived here all their lives and did so much for the country? On my first visit here I knew nothing of this, only that they were kind, loving, family people who showed much generosity and hospitality to a new arrival.

Next morning we said 'Goodbye', promised to visit them at Shiwa and drove north. It was a long drive but a good road, we reached our destination late in the afternoon. We branched off into a much used red dirt track and I had my first sight of the new housing estate. I viewed the neat row of tiny white bungalow, just as Simon must have done, with some dismay. There is no shortage of land here, who then had thought this up, or was it for economy. There was no fencing and I soon learned that anything left outside at night disappeared. A pity because an enormous ugly fence was shortly erected.

The family were there to greet me and show me this dolls' house, the swimming pool was up and took up most of the garden, it was much in demand for it was the only one for miles and the weather was hot. It was the season of the small rains which meant unexpected and very heavy showers which turned the earth into a sea of mud. Later these houses had extensions and a swimming pool, there was also a pool in the Irish compound but this was, as yet undiscovered by the family.

The house consisted of one living room, two little bedrooms, the office where I was to sleep and a kitchen made for someone who didn't expect to spend time there or possibly an anorexic dwarf. Considering the size of many African women it certainly wasn't built for them. This kitchen was also a passage, the back door being here leading to the bush back garden. There was a tiny bathroom squeezed in between the office and the kitchen, when all were at home with the dog, the cat and all the friends Liz and Adam had made, including those just coming to see the baby, it was concentrated bedlam. I could see Simon was restless, it held so little scope. Jennie, as usual, was coping well but now she had Mother-in-law to add to her problems. I couldn't help thinking she looked a little strained.

The office housed all the usual equipment but none of it barked or meowed or even screamed. I made myself as small as possible and enquired about this 'something bigger'.

"Its on the hill the other side of town, the tenants have gone back to England. I met them in Lusaka and promised to look after their dog only if I could have the house, they were going to mention my name to the landlord. I also said I'd take on their cook and their gardener but I can's pay them until I've signed the lease. Meanwhile squatters have moved in, the two men are upset, no job no money."

It sounded a bit vague which is why I made myself at home, tried to help and hoped for better things.

Our neighbours were close so it was fortunate that we were already friends, some we had met in Norway. Harry and Maureen were on one side and Thor and Christina with their family next but one on the other side with an empty house between. This awaited the economist and his teacher wife who was to take over the school. Everyone came in for swims so it was cheerful and noisy.

Simon came in in an excited mood.

"I've met the Chief of the district," he told us, "He knows the owner. Harry's going down to Lusaka, I'm going with him to get this thing settled."

"Can I go and see the place?" I asked equally excited.

"No," he replied, "Wait until I get back and it's settled. "Don't interfere," he added rather nastily, I thought.

As if I would.

"Are you pleased?" I asked Jennie when he had gone. "Do you like the house?"

"I've not seen it," she admitted. "Not until I know for sure. It's another move," she sighed.

I was not so patient as Jennie, I longed to have a look at it. I then realized Simon had left both vehicle and driver, Mark, behind.

Mark now called to see if he could do anything for us. I didn't wait for Jennie.

"Drive me over there to the new house," I said.

Mark looked doubtful but accepted Mama's word as law so we went.

The bungalow was well out of town and the way was full of twists and turns on pot-holed dirt roads through numerous small holdings of maize and beans and bright with nasturtiums, marigolds and bougainvillaea. There were bananas and mango trees and others I did not recognize. The houses varied from small shacks to good sized houses, the people were friendly and waved as we went by.

I fell in love with the place immediately, I suppose it could best be described as 'Old Colonial'. It was a long low bungalow with a veranda, the back was just as attractive as the front and the whole had a spacious and welcoming appearances if it longed to be inhabited, at the moment it had a lonely deserted look. The tenants who had been living there were people with a temporary outlook and it now looked neglected, perhaps not intentionally, maybe it just wasn't home to them. An attempt had been made to create an English garden so it was nostalgic rather than beautiful, the roses were miserable specimens in contrast to the African blooms which still managed to flourish. An orange and lemon grove to one side of the bungalow would, I felt sure, soon regain its productive life once Simon got his hands on it. There seemed to be no definite boundaries except on one side, on two sides were roads and the back garden was part of the scenery.

Mark and I climbed down from the truck as two men came running round the side of the bungalow. They spoke to Mark but the conversation being in Bemba it was only the disappearance of anxiety and the wide grins indicating hope that gave me an understanding of the palaver.

My hand was shaken and I was conducted with all ceremony into the house which had the same stagnant look as the garden, luckily the ants had not yet moved in.

There was nothing wrong with the house, it just had that unlived in look which was not improved by some dilapidated bits of furniture that the former tenants had left behind. Simon had promised, if he managed to rent the property, to buy these bits but I could imagine a nice heap outside with a 'help yourself' notice written on it.

The handsome young houseman, William, was a Tanzanian.
He was living in the house and had managed to keep the squatters
outside. I was already seeing the place as it would be once Simon
and Jennie moved in. There was a large entrance hall, a sitting room
the full breadth of the house with French windows to the back
garden, a dining room and kitchen, an office and cloakroom and a
dividing door to the sleeping quarters. Here there were three good
bedrooms and a bathroom and beyond a separate lockable big
bedroom with its own bathroom.

What possibilities this place had, it would soon lose that
makeshift, impermanent feel. Already I had a feeling of belonging.
I went outside where the squatters camp lay untidily under a beautiful
fig tree. They had a rough shelter and their goods were scattered
about them, when it rained, which it did often as this was the season
of the small rains, they took shelter in a doorless garage. William
and Luke looked on disapprovingly, the squatters were not popular,
either here or in the district, they didn't belong as they came from
another tribe and were distrusted.

As the men's faces brightened so those of the squatters became
gloomy. It was obvious that my presence was take as a confirmation
of the family's forthcoming occupation which meant jobs and
prosperity. William brought tea while I walked around hoping I
hadn't raised expectations needlessly, but if I knew Simon I didn't
think I had.

Mark was helping me back into the truck when Luke appeared
carrying a gift of strawberries in a home-made leaf basket.

"For you," William told him to say, but I felt it was more than
that, that Luke thought these were ours by right.

To the men the beginning of a new order, to me it was a good
omen.

I gave them to Jennie when I returned. "They're yours, it's your
house and you'll love it."

And she did of course.

Simon arrived triumphant.

"It's all settled," he said, "Now let's go and look at it."

Jennie didn't tell on me so I admitted to a previous short visit,
he wasn't listening, he was so busy thinking up the next course of
action and anxious to get going on it.

We were welcomed as before, a loaded lorry appeared as if from nowhere with, as Simon explained, 'a few things I bought in Lusaka'.

The empty lorry was then 'offered' to the squatters, they and their goods were piled onto it and waved off. They seemed happy to go, their life in unknown territory had been precarious, their departure was reason for celebration.

The bungalow looked less desolate with the family running around in it, the children found the garden and were playing with Luke, sightseers had appeared, we were already a centre of interest and speculation.

"It still looks a bit empty," said Simon as we all walked around, mentally furnishing, decorating, measuring, arranging or shopping. Liz and Adam come in from the garden to decide on their bedrooms, imaginations put up shelves and saw it as it would be.

We went into the garden escorted by Luke and found bananas, paw paw, passion fruit, mangos and a magnificent asparagus bed as well as the strawberry bed. The boundaries were non-existent. Simon was worried, if you do keep chickens or for that matter any livestock or children's pets it's as well to have a fence. We were all quiet on the way home, thinking, perhaps, of what it would be like to live here. This was an exciting week for next day Simon and Jennie's own car arrived. It had been ordered some time ago but had now been driven up from Dar es Salaam. It was roomy and red, it was also filthy and still covered in bits of wrapping paper. The cleaning of it was a noisy and rewarding operation. It was greatly admired. "We'll all go down to Lusaka in it," said Simon to Jennie, "Harry and Maureen were talking of going down to shop, we can do our Christmas shopping as well as get a few things you may need for the house. I'll find some cheap accommodation."

I noted the 'you', I could see Simon needed plenty of things for the house.

"We can go in convoy," he added.

It wasn't much of a convoy, Harry and Maureen rushed on ahead. Not for them cheap family accommodation, there were only two of them and they intended to have the best. And the best hotel it was, with shops and live crocodiles in the cafe pool, whereas ours was n a sleazier part of town behind a corrugated iron fence with a rickety gate and a doubtful guard. In some ways it reminded me of the prison back home but I made no remark, after all Simon was paying, there were six of us and, if his economy drive meant this, who was I to grumble. Once through the gates it looked a bit better although basic. Simon cheerfully told us all how much we were going to enjoy it and I felt sure I could manage in my hut in spite of the grubby floor, broken furniture and cracked basin. I turned on the one tap and a brown liquid emerged looking a little like the lower reaches of a contaminated river. There was no mosquito net and no air conditioning, however there was a television set and I now turned this on in a half-hearted fashion more out of interest than expectation. To my great surprise an episode of the latest Barbara Taylor Bradford serial appeared on the screen. Stunned, for I hadn't seen it, I was prepared to forego the essentials of life. So I dumped my luggage, put my feet up on the bed and prepared to make the best of things.

It was not to be. Simon appeared having been on the trail of food and found the kitchen conditions much the same as those in the chalets. He'd returned to find Jennie on the verge of tears with smelly nappies, the children hungry and miserable and the baby crying.

"Pack up," he now said to me, "We're leaving, hang economy, we're going to the Intercontinental."

I hadn't unpacked being too engrossed in 'The Woman of Substance' which I was reluctant to leave being unsure if I should find it anywhere else, I longed to know, but never shall, if some magical crossing of wires had produced it in my hut. Also I thought I'd caught a glimpse of a swimming pool but there probably wasn't any water in it.

Conditions were rather different in the Intercontinental where things often work, where there's a magnificent pool and rooms with air-conditioning. We had rooms with connecting doors and all facilities. Jennie fed the baby who promptly fell asleep and she and Simon departed to start the shopping.

"I could do with a cup of tea," I said to Liz, there was only a water jug.

Liz was, and still is, full of confidence, pressing the right buttons she called for room service. She ordered tea and said "Yes, please," with increasing enthusiasm to questions I couldn't hear. Soon there was a knock on the door and a waiter with a loaded trolley appeared, his main object was for me to vote for him as 'employee of the month' and I was only too willing to do this for him before we fell upon this unexpected feast. Unexpected to me, I feel sure Liz knew exactly what was coming. Tea, sandwiches, cakes, we made short work of it before Simon returned hoping that he would not notice the extra expense and question the necessity for afternoon tea.

"Where's your shopping?" I asked Simon when they returned to the hotel.

"A lorry will come up with a few things," he replied vaguely, "It'll come up next weekend and then we'll move."

Oh! another lorry load and a useful extra lorry.

Jennie and I did some Christmas shopping next morning while the others settled themselves by the pool. I wanted to see something of the town and visit the copper shops, I had already done my present buying back home. Last year's remnants of tatty decorations in the African heat is not conducive to festive shopping. We were glad to join the others at the poolside before heading North once more.

Back home we had new neighbours. Its an odd feeling looking back on a first meeting with people who have since become close friends. Matthew was the teams economist and his wife, Heather, was to take over the school. The children, Judith, James and Mary, soon made friends with Liz and Adam. Mary was only a little bit older than baby Peter. It was such a happy meeting that they were sorry to hear that we, and the swimming pool, were moving so soon, they were sympathetic however as they too were wondering how they were going to fit into the tiny villa. They promised to visit us frequently and I could see they were already planning an extension. Later most of this row of houses were improved and extended as the only happy housewife was a minute Japanese lady with no family.

The dog died in the night, it was very old, I think it had been ill long before we took it in but a promise is a promise and we didn't like to ask the vet to put it down. Jennie and I had taken it to the vet several times but old age is not really curable. Simon found it cold that morning and buried it in a bush grave, all the local children came and put flowers on it. It probably became an important shrine, I am quite sure the children were unaware of what it was.

Saturday came, the day of the move. I am, fortunately, an early riser and had found it a good time to squeeze into the kitchen when no-one else was about in order to make and enjoy my first cup of tea.

"There'll be plenty of helpers," Simon had said, "The men like to earn a little overtime."

I heard a noise, looked out and saw a piled up lorry with two men cheerfully waving to any interested party. When I next looked there were six men and this increased to ten in a very short time.

I knocked on Simon and Jennie's door.

"The lorry's here, what shall I do?"

"Tell them to start moving things," replied Simon. I swear he turned over.

Jennie got up hastily. I hung onto the tea making equipment.

The lorry already looked top-heavy but in Africa anything is possible and even a square inch can accommodate another piece of furniture.

Simon stuck his head out of the window and shouted encouraging directions.

It had rained and everything in the lorry was very wet, it was mostly office furniture but our own personal shopping had been added at the last minute and was wettest of all.

Some more men arrived to turn the water off, they were mending a leak they said. To us it no longer mattered.

The sun came out.

We dressed and breakfasted hastily. Simon went off with the lorry "to start the other end," and Jennie and I prepared to finish this one.

Our neighbours arrived to see if they could help by having the children. Liz went off happily but Adam, upset by the turmoil and unsure what was happening or why, hid behind the car and refused to go. The baby, having been fed earlier, slept on.

The rain started again and came down, as only tropical rain can, in drenching floods.

Simon arrived back this time with a tractor and trailer, it was soon loaded up, Adam cheerfully went with his father, Jennie and I were left, thankfully with the tea things.

It was afternoon before the last load left. It consisted of Jennie and Jennie's car, Liz, Adam, who had been going back and forth on reassuring journeys, and me. We nearly forgot the baby and the cat was loose in the solid mass of goods in the car. We knew it was there as there was an occasional small meow. I was glad to go, I know I was clutching the teapot but there was no water.

Simon was directing things at the other end, his office was well arranged and drying out. William was trying to provide his new employers with something worthy of the occasion such as baked beans on toast. We were too tired to care, we fitted up beds, Simon paid off the men, told the faithful William to take a couple of days off and we called it a day.

Next day was Sunday and theoretically a day of rest, the early arrival of painters, carpenters and hangers on hopeful of an unexpected handout soon put the idea of relaxation out of our minds. It was a wonderful house with its door to the bedrooms where one could find peace. The whole house was still a bit unfurnished, we had enough beds and bedding, everyone had somewhere to sit and there was the television set, even if the programmes were not as good as 'the set'. A rug spread out on the concrete floor helped to create less of a 'we're just passing through' look.

In the office and in the kitchen things were very different. The office furniture having dried out a complete study had grown around it, the computer, the word-processor, books, shelves, files and filing cabinet were all there. I don't know where it had all come from but Simon viewed his domain with smug satisfaction.

He then turned his attention to the kitchen. This large bare dreary looking workplace first needed a coat of paint, Simon had collected two painters and an excellent carpenter, there were, of course, the usual helpers carrying bits of wood or paint or merely standing by with advice. William would not return until Monday and Simon was determined to provide him too with a high quality area worthy of a good cook. In the other small house there had been no room for the equipment we had all enthused over in London, this now came out of store and arranged to Jennie's satisfaction. With everything in its place it was a cook's gleaming paradise.

Simon again paid off the men and again there seemed to be more people in the wages queue than there had been working, consequently there were a few flare-ups, probably the Bemba equivalent of "No, you didn't", "Yes, I did", but it all ended peacefully with goodwill all round. Simon knew his workforce but I don't think anyone went away empty handed even the small boy who had been holding a paint brush for his Dad. Extra cash was a welcome bonus for some of these men, one of whom admitted to having ten children. There were great guffaws of laughter when Simon theatrically waved a sharp knife saying he'd soon put an end to that. Many of the men supported other relatives besides their own immediate family, I assumed, as they all had Christian names, that they were Christians with only one wife but there can be many translations of the idea and I didn't like to ask, the word 'brother' too can be used loosely and may not mean a direct relationship. 'Cousin' is even vaguer.

I was glad I was up early next morning and able to witness William's entrance, I shall never forget his face, no actor could have produced that look of wonderment. In disbelief he walked round touching everything. I suppose to make sure it was real. Even the dirty pipes under the sink were now tidily boxed in. It was a transformation and one that William found it difficult to take in. The rest of the house looked different and more homely with toys lying about. It was clean, newly painted and more cheerful, but it was the kitchen that bore no relation to its appearance two days ago.

It took William several days to recover from the drama but then he settled down to enjoy himself and with such facilities and Jennie to help him, he was determined to make this his career, perhaps later to go into hotel work in his own country of Tanzania. He spoke three languages, his own, Swahili, Bemba and English, he was anxious to learn French and while I was there we started on this.

There were quite a few people at the back door that first morning along with most of the local dogs. Jennie took on a smiling cheerful girl called Rose to help with the baby and washing and Simon took on a boy to help Luke in the garden. The openness of the place and the dogs made the boundary question and fencing of primary importance. We also discovered we had peacocks in one corner of the grounds.

"Yes, they're ours," said Simon casually. "I thought they'd look nice wandering about the lawn." He was thinking, no doubt, of our local landowners estate. "We must fence the place in," he added as he saw the poor cat sitting on the roof.

"I'll go and talk to the chief now," he said, "Perhaps I'll take the car and fetch him. Could you make it something of an occasion?"

We dressed up, me in one of those just-in-case dresses popped into my luggage at the last moment and Jennie found a clean shirt.

The Chief arrived, we made it as ceremonial as we could. The 'staff' lined up, we didn't recognize some of them but this was not the time for quibbling. We realized that excitements were few around here and no-one wanted to miss the fun.

Jennie and I sat on the veranda in state while the boundary walking proceeded, the Chief was so obviously enjoying his accepted status and this moment of his power we wanted to be sure he got the most out of it. He would return to the veranda where William would serve coffee.

All went well and when the ritual was over the Chief stood to make a speech. This was accompanied by much hand clapping for emphasis on his part, the speech was in Bemba so he translated for us.

"I am telling them that you are good people and no-one must ever steal from you."

We thanked him, everyone drifted away and Simon drove him home, returning with rolls of wire fencing because, as he said, "everyone means well but it's just as well to be on the safe side."

He then brought out two puppies which the children fell on with delight.

"They'll grow up to be guard dogs," he said. What he didn't know at the time was that these two adorable bundles would grow up to kill anything in sight, or try to.

The fencing soon went up, the skinny African mongrels were on the outside and the cat came down from the roof.

CHAPTER 10

With all this domesticity, ours and observing that of our neighbours, there was little time for safaris on this first visit of mine to Zambia. We were well settled in for Christmas, word went around, through Harry, that we were going to have the feast in our big room and everyone offered either furniture or food or both. William refused to have the day off, the previous tenants never having been over-generous with the food, guests had been rare. Africans love a party and William wasn't going to miss it, not only that the kitchen was his pride and joy and he was going to be the centre of it. If there was to be a later barbecue, as seemed possible, he was determined to be presiding over it. To our surprise Luke turned up as well, this behaviour was not entirely disinterested, there would be tips and generous leftovers.

It seemed to us to be a great celebration but it was very tame compared with the office party which Simon and Jennie agreed would be held in this spacious house. It was unlike any office party I had ever attended, heard of, or imagined. The Europeans departed early when the African music started and the dancing began. There were whoops of rollicking laughter when my new friends tried to teach me that wonderful hip-swaying movements that the Africans have. I found it hard to imitate and my stiff white gyrations only produced guffaws of fat laughter, I decided I hadn't the bottom for it. Simon called a halt to the party when most of the participants were laid out in the grounds or asleep on various bits of furniture, some were crying - loud body-rocking sobs for what reason I never discovered. Long before this Jennie and I and the children had cloistered ourselves in the shut off bedroom part of the house, taking with us the more expensive drink. This had to last so we hid it away, we left them the home brew.

The festivities over we found it was not all fun and games on the hill; we had water problems. A lot of the inhabitants seemed to accept the carrying of water for long distances on their heads. Simon wanted better things.

"We've two bathrooms, three loos, a wonderful clean kitchen with sink, a garden hose and a pool waiting to be erected, none of it much use without water."

We agreed with him so he set himself the task of finding the nearest reservoir and improving the situation.

"He didn't mention the washing machine," said Jennie as we viewed the growing pile of dirty clothes and the rainwater ran out.

I don't know how he managed it but soon the whole district was enjoying a good water supply and no longer depended upon rain falling into the tank on the roof or, in some cases, rain falling and no tank on the roof and going without if unprepared to walk to the nearest town tap. Necessity now satisfied, Simon turned his attention to leisure activities so the pool went up and was filled. We became popular.

This trip had been mainly domestic but I was reluctant to leave, I'd seen very little of the country which I'd heard spoken of as the 'real Africa'.

"Next time," said Simon, "There's Lake Tanganyika, we can camp there at Ndole Bay, it's in Nsumba National Park so it should have wildlife, there's Malawi and the Nyika Plateau, the Copper Belt should be interesting if not beautiful, there's ....."

He didn't finish but my mind was wandering and my mouth watering at the thought of these future treats.

So it was 'Goodbye' again and I departed with the knowledge that my return would be to this happy, busy place where the family were settled and thriving.

Summer is hardly over when Christmas starts in the UK. For once I was thankful for I was able to stretch out my Christmas shopping and when the time came again for my departure I had bought all my presents. I had also 'done' my Christmas cards. I had reached the time when I was counting the days when I was struck down by flu - a particularly virulent germ that year. I packed feverishly in case I became worse and lost all powers of thought. Should I make it? If on the morning of my departure I was incapable of standing I would give up the idea. The morning came, I felt shaky but roadworthy. It was snowing hard. My travelling over the years had increased my confidence. "Nothing to it" I told myself, "It's easy when you come to it."

It couldn't last.

Tom, reluctantly, got out the car and agreed to try to reach a station which we did eventually. Not the one we were aiming at but a coastal station along a flat coastal road, it was a terminal and a train awaited, it could only go one way. Tom drove off hastily "in case it got worse." I only hoped it wouldn't as I only had a small flask to keep me going. There was no indication that the train would move but several passengers boarded it and hope returned. Eventually it managed to reach Bournemouth where we were told it couldn't go any further but another might possibly come from another direction. The passengers had become a united group by this time and we all congregated in the station refreshment room, our friendliness based perhaps on the fact that we had a common enemy. One young man was going to Australia, most of the group had heard of this but Zambia - it was like going to the moon.

"Is it anywhere near Rhodesia?" someone asked.

I reached Heathrow at last but still all was not plain sailing, the aeroplane appeared to be missing and no-one knew what had happened to it.

Was my whole journey going to be full of setbacks?

It was well after midnight and I was definitely flagging when we were told that we could have a free meal and hotels would be found for us. The first class passengers and then the families were fixed up before the economy single people who were put three to a room. As I approached the desk for my reservation I was flanked by two ladies, a gentle Indian woman and a pretty travelling-alone Danish girl. I think they chose me because I looked safe and, of course, motherly, but I was worried for I still felt a little light-headed and wondered if I was still infectious. We were a threesome from that moment on, had our meals together and shared a room. Chance could have brought me far less amiable companions, and I had not met up with Victoria Wood.

We were called early as room on a flight had been found for us.

There was no Simon at the airport to meet me at the other end, he had given up hope and gone home.

With little sleep, the remains of flu and full of worry as to what I should do, I had little patience with the customs officials. The luggage arrived in a higgledy piggledy pile up on benches or on the floor, endless forms were handed out. I broke through the barriers and demanded help. I grabbed the nearest taxi driver and insisted that he be allowed through to get my luggage, he looked terrified. I shoved the papers back at the astounded officer, refused to pay the money he demanded and followed my luggage which was legging it at full speed with the taxi driver who obviously expected shots at any minute. Nobody fired.

"The best hotel in town," I said. No need to tell him to go fast.

I had from him the information, at last, as to what had happened to the lost plane. A baggage carrier had hit it and it had never taken off.

"It was buggered," he explained. In Africa this is a normal word for broken. I had remonstrated with Simon the previous year when Adam used it about one of his toys.

"That's right," Simon had said, "it was buggered." What's the use!

I found there was a message for me at the hotel desk, Simon had anticipated what I would do. The message read - "Couldn't wait, flight booked 07.30, will meet you at airport other end."

"Can you be here early in the morning?" I asked my new devoted taxi driver.

"Yes, Yes," he said, giving a bow full of hope and visualizing a good Christmas.

I lay on my bed too tired to eat or drink and too confused to remember what was packed where.

The phone rang, it was my early call, I ordered tea, tea would revive me for I was little refreshed by the brief sleep.

There was not only no tea, there was no electricity, no lifts and apparently there were no men. I dragged my luggage down some steep concrete back stairs and arrived at the reception desk to find no-one there. A tray of someone's tea was sitting invitingly on the desk, it could have been mine, I didn't ask, I wanted tea and there it way. I enjoyed it. My now more cheerful taxi man arrived and agreed to accept dollars, I know I overpaid him but he was there when I needed him. I suspected his kwacha - dollar exchange rate would have been higher than mine.

I was in time for the domestic flight, the departure part of the airport was a great deal better than the arrival part and the small aircraft that took me north on the last part of my journey was waiting on the tarmac. The plane was full of businessmen who alighted at a stop for the copper belt. It looked very uninteresting. One man came back looking worried.

"This is the end," he explained, "It stops here."

"Surely not," I said, looking for my ticket, could I have made a mistake. "I'm going to . . ."

"Oh! THERE," he said scornfully, he looked puzzled trying to 'place' me. A missionary perhaps, or, as I hoped, a great traveller that he should have recognized.

And so I arrived at last at, to me, the perfect airport, it has or had one runway and a couple of huts. Everyone collected there to watch with wonder and delight the tiny spec in the distance draw nearer and become a real live aeroplane. It was an exciting as well as a social occasion, gossip was exchanged, invitations were given and accepted, trips and ideas were discussed.

The family were there to meet me, Adam hiding and shyly peeping out from behind Jennie but Elizabeth came running across to greet me. It was that sort of airport.

Jennie and Heather were going down to Lusaka on the return flight to do some Christmas shopping and have a short break from their families, Heather was hoping to get some equipment for the school. There was just time for lunch and a quick exchange of news before they took off again. Simon was reassuring Jennie that he had everything in hand and all would be well. The children and I now had a few days to get to know each other again. Peter was walking now but that first night he was none too happy without his mother. He started to cry, Simon found he had work to do elsewhere and disappeared. I seemed unable to pacify Peter and Lizzie got out of bed with a deep sigh, looked reproachfully at me as if it was my fault and took him into bed with her, finding this inadequate even for two small people she determinedly took him into her parents bed. Adam trailed behind dragging various bits of blanket and toys, they shut the door. I was exhausted and fell asleep so have no idea of Simon's reactions when he returned, perhaps he didn't notice, it was a quiet house and a big bed.

After this all ran smoothly but we were all glad to see Jennie when she returned.

There were changes of course; the dogs had grown as well as the children. The children's growth hadn't changed them much but the two delightful puppies were now two savage dogs bent on destroying anything that crossed their paths. The peacocks no longer strutted proudly across the lawn, they were in an enclosure and heaven help them if they decided that the grass was greener on the other side. Their frequent escape meant that all and sundry, led by William and Luke, (there always appeared to be a lot of sundry) shouted, waved whatever they could find to make the occasion more impressive and joined in this enjoyable and theatrical game.

Simon had come to an agreement with the local population. If the smallholders' chickens who scratched around for their own living strayed inside our fence they were fair game, but, if the dogs strayed outside and killed Simon paid up with no argument. Everyone agreed it was a fair arrangement. People were another matter and unknown visitors had to be escorted in. Once inside they were accepted and safe. We had no burglaries other than the loss of some chickens where the fence had been breached in the far corner of the garden. In spite of this loss there were plenty of eggs.

There were now three cats all of whom lived hazardous lives but were safe up trees or on the roof.

The swimming pool was well used, and the veranda had grown. A new and better barbecue had been built. There was a permanent happy feeling to the place.

A nursery group now gathered in the big entrance hall which made a wonderful school room. Starting off as a few Mothers with Toddlers, it had now become a well organized enterprise. With Jennie away I had an immediate occupation.

Simon had decided to grow coffee and there were hundreds of small healthy looking plants, seed was germinating under a sack, when I lifted this out shot a snake, after that I wasn't too keen on coffee growing. In later years this ground grew sunflowers which were much prettier than coffee and were a good source of chicken feed.

"Why are you growing coffee?" I asked Simon, "It isn't likely that you will get to a harvesting stage."

"I'm selling the plants," he explained. "If anyone comes for them get Luke to pack them up." He mentioned the price in Kwacha, they weren't expensive. I was delighted when a woman arrived to buy. At last I was, as a saleswoman, justifying my existence.

"Certainly," I said, full of hope and thinking in terms of lorry loads, "How many?"

"Thirty," she replied. Obviously she wasn't going in to it in a big way and I wasn't helping to make the family fortune.

"We're going to have the Christmas party here again," said Jennie, "Its expected of us, it will become a tradition if we're here long enough."

"No-one else will have the office party either," said Simon, "The last one was talked about for weeks."

I hastily hid my large bottle of duty-free whisky, it had to last a long time.

"But," said Simon, "After that we're going camping by Lake Tanganika and Adam and I are going fishing."

Adam looked surprised as well he might but he was now three and a bit and if Dad said so it was so. Everyone else thought this a good idea and as there was a camp site beside the lake it was decided that it could be a camping party and the idea flourished.

The Christmas dinner was much enlivened this year by an addition of an Italian friend of Simon and Jennies. Roberto sang and his rich well-lubricated Italian voice added a robust note at every possible moment throughout the meal. Next day he called to apologize.

"No need," I told him, "We loved every minute of it."

He was a regular visitor, his wife was in Rome as she refused to live in, "an uncivilized country like Zambia". Roberto's work was here but he was obviously lonely and called regularly. He was even teaching some Italian to William. If Jennie wasn't there he talked, sang, drank coffee, bought eggs and departed happily. He refused to come camping with us, he was always immaculately dressed and I could see he thought it a barbaric idea.

The highlight of Christmas was the nursery group's Nativity play. Jennie put this on to entertain the parents. No need here to black in one of the Kings. Adam was a King and led the three onto the makeshift stage. When he saw he had an audience he went into reverse and they all landed in a heap. The audience loved it.

Christmas over a very much larger party than we had first intended, left for Ndole Bay.

It was a perfect spot but there were, I now think, too many of us and the site had not been properly fitted up, there was a water tap but no electricity. Who needs water when the lake was so beautiful and Harry could be depended upon for early warnings of crocs or water snakes. He put up my tent for me near to the water tap and under the nests of some beautiful weaver birds. I had a view of the sparkling lake and I was for a short time perfectly happy. But then, another family in the party whose names I have forgotten, put up their tent between me and the lake and facing the other way, they had a baby and the mother spent the whole of her time at the tap washing out nappies. I joined the others on the beach, wondering why it needed nappies in such a place as this.

We did what we could with the various lamps we had to light our supper around the camp fire, it was decided to leave clearing up and washing up until morning. As an early riser I found this to have been a mistake. It had rained, we had been raided by monkeys and what had been a 'bit of a mess' was, now, a disastrous mess. Regretting my early start but needing a cup of tea I set about the clearing up; most of the tents were set up in the clearing where the fire and meal had been so I made as much noise as I could packing up dishes and shoving away the monkeys. One by one the other campers joined me. Next night the hotel manager, who also managed the camp site, brought electricity, with plenty of wires and bulbs hung in trees, to us. We only stayed two days and even Simon thought that there had been too many of us, especially when he had spent most of the time he had wanted to spend fishing on the edge of the lake washing up. "We'll come on our own," he said, "We can take a hut, have some meals in the restaurant and Adam and I can go fishing at last."

The restaurant idea was a good one, I had found morning tea up there and had sat in the pleasant open-to-the-air dining room and enjoyed the peace. His time there was not wasted for he found nearby farmers willing to join his scheme and thus ensured some more visits. We also went with him when he had work near the Nyika Plateau in the north. It was still school holidays and Jennie agreed that we could all go, the guest houses were good and very reasonable. It was country both she and I wanted to see.

"Bring passports," said Simon, "We might go over the border to Malawi."

I loved the simplicity of the first guest house, it was a bring your own food type, it was basic, clean and the view was wonderful. Wandering around I found many beautiful wild flowers including orchids. We booked a return visit and crossed into Malawi. The border posts always have young soldiers with guns, Simon insisted that they had no ammunition and not to worry.

"Without ammo these are only toys but they are only boys and they like to have them, no-one can afford ammunition, besides it's dangerous," he said.

We were stopped this time and several armed young men with hats at arrogant angles approached.

"You have papers?" one asked, looking at the vehicle and trying to place us.

"Of course," said Simon, "I'm with the government."

We handed over passports and smiled encouragingly. I'm not sure that they can all read but this one was an enthusiastic reader and took some time over my passport. It is, by now, an interesting document full of stamps from far off places.

"Teacher?" he asks, "You find me pen-friend in England?"

"Certainly," I reply and take his name and address. Who knows perhaps my student Paul would like a Zambian pen-friend. I could hardly suggest changing names with a prison inmate.

We then stretched our legs in the new country, waved to the collecting crowd and drove off. Wherever we went the children's bright hair usually aroused a good deal of interest.

We saw something of Malawi as we drove towards the lake. We stopped to shop and there seemed more in the shops here than in Zambia. We bought enough food to last us for we were not sure what sort of accommodation we should find.

We had views of the beautiful lake as we approached it and we found a quiet and moderately priced motel, here we took two lakeside huts which stood on a sandy beach beneath palm trees. On the side we were on the lake is known as Lake Malawi but other countries border onto it, I have no idea what it is called on the Mozambique side. I had now visited many of the Rift Valley lakes from Turkann southwards, perhaps in time, who knows, I may get to visit them all.

We spent two days here, the food wasn't spectacular and some crisps we bought seemed to permeate the whole of the children's bodies, Simon said I imagined it but Adam particularly seemed to have absorbed some strange animal fat.

Malawi was, and I hope still is, mindful of its wildlife heritage, the National Parks are well maintained and the camps are good.

As we made our way back to the Nyika Plateau and home, the

rain started. It rained, heavy, tropical, drenching rain, it grew dark, the camp looked anything but inviting. It appeared to be washed out, water was flooding through it. Not a soul was in sight. The thought of putting up tents in this quagmire with the rain still pouring down was a depressing one, it was surprisingly cold and we had food to unpack and cook. A silence descended upon us, even Simon seemed despondent and failed to tell us that we should enjoy it.

"We'll try the hutted camp," he said, "We might be lucky, if not we'll have to sleep in the car.

We were lucky, there was one empty hut, they were lovely wooden huts in beautiful forest surroundings. What bliss it was to come in out of the rain to this snug apartment. A man arrived to 'do' for us, this entailed lighting the fire and lamps and also to cook. Thee was no electricity and we were expected to provide our own food. Luckily we had expected to camp and had plenty. The inside of this delightful bungalow was also of wood, we sat round a huge wooden table on wooden benches and regained our feeling of well-being.

The next morning was sunny, cool and pleasant, the rain had stopped. This cabin among the fir trees made me think of Scotland and I set off on an early stroll.

I heard a shout, I turned, the shouter didn't look like a Scot.

"Memsahib," he called, "Go back ... leopard."

So it wasn't Scotland and although I had never seen a leopard I took his advice and retreated within our fence. I didn't wish my first sight of this animal to be my last.

Our return journey was uneventful and all was normal back home, if you can call the usual African dramas normal. The dogs and cats were well and if we were a few chickens less it was not an affair worth going into because the real truth would never be revealed.

Harry rushed over to keep us up-to-date with the local news, who was ill, who had come and who had departed.

Term started, and I entertained Roberto, walked the dogs round and round the garden and went shopping in the not very foodwise, exciting market. There were plenty of people with not much to sell. Simon had suggested to Luke that he started a stall with our surplus garden produce but either he didn't understand or, more likely, couldn't be bothered for he never did so.

CHAPTER 11

We had been back home for a week when Simon came in rather earlier than usual.

"Were you serious about wanting to go on the 'Tanzam'," he enquired.

The Tanzam is the railway that runs the length of Zambia and Tanzania to the coast at Dar es Salaam.

"I am serious," I replied, for I am always serious about my travelling and especially about railways.

"I have to go that way and possibly to Nairobi," he said. "It may take a little longer but we may as well try it out as I don't want to take the car, there are too many taxes at the borders and flying is worse. I'm told the train goes on Tuesday so ..."

I interrupted him.

"What shall I take?" I asked for I was already mentally packing.

"Any old thing," he said, male like, "And your sleeping bag. It says food on the train but ... be on the safe side - perhaps - and a thermos." Later we were glad we had been on the 'safe side'.

"There's a boat from Dar to Mombasa," I now told Simon, it was a route I'd researched. "And from Mombasa we could take the train to Nairobi."

"All the same, I'll get return tickets," he replied firmly.

Tuesday came, Simon went to the station early.

"It'll be in tonight," he informed me. "Be ready about six."

A friend of Jennie's came in to coffee, she too had heard about the boat but, she said, avoid the bus.

I agreed to avoid the bus.

Later Simon came in and said the train would go on Wednesday, possibly, but certainly not tonight. He had not managed to book seats as there was no booking staff and the phone wasn't working. I wondered if the train was mythical although I had heard distant sounds of a railway.

But Simon was still in optimistic mood and, on Wednesday, we both went to the station, there was no train but rumour had it that it might arrive tomorrow. We went home. Later Simon returned alone to the station, found a booking clerk, and booked, hopefully return tickets. They had the numbers of our sleeping berths and our carriage on them, the trip began to become reality.

"Tomorrow at 7.00 am," he informed me on his return.

I said I'd be ready and Jennie rushed us to the station before school started. The station is a very fine building some way out of town and we had plenty of time to admire it before the train arrived at half-past nine.

We looked for our carriage and numbered sleeping berths but these did not appear to exist, we walked with increasing frustration with the usual interested spectators up and down the train, we were eventually bundled into a compartment that looked moderately empty. Our fellow passengers disappeared one by one perhaps not liking the look of us. One girl, fast asleep, did not notice the general exodus.

"Not well," a friend of hers informed us. When she awoke she looked at us in dismay, gathered up her belongings and departed hastily to join her mates.

Perhaps at one time this had been a fine express and still could be. Sadly now, it was neglected and had obviously deteriorated. It wasn't very clean, Simon decided to check the loos. He said he though the 'footsteps' type was marginally the better of the two sorts.

"The seat one is so disgusting," he said, "It's better not to consider sitting down".

I went to look. The 'footsteps' type consisted of a hole in the floor but I survived the other one by trying not to breathe. I had learned to travel with disposable seat covers. There was no water.

These were minor troubles compared to the excitement of the journey, the scenery, real Africa, the hills, the valleys, the animals and the lively stations. It was stimulating and exhilarating.

I was glad of the thermos but if I ever travel that way again I should take water too and a camping stove. Food was no problem for at the various stops an excited vibrant crowd of sellers scrambled around the train, hanging on to bits of it, shouting and waving hands and trays of goodies. Simon loves these curious looking goods but I prefer something with a removable skin and there were plenty of bananas. We didn't try the train food. I asked one girl what it was like and she replied, "Good, good." "But what is it?" I asked.

"Nshima," she replied. This porridge-like meal is not to my liking.

There was coke at the stations so we were not without drinks. It isn't the best liquid in which to wash and does not, to my way of thinking, replace a good cup of tea.

The border brought another excitement, there were strange new and different shouts, larger more purposeful men pushed onto the train, shouting and waving bits of paper. They were money changers, we hastily bought enough Tanzanian shillings to last us until we reached Dar es Salaam. This whole noisy, rushed scene ended with a surprising suddenness. One minute these men were there and next they were gone.

"What's happening and why?" I asked Simon. He was leaning out of the window and I felt he should know. He sat down with a knowing "Ah ha!" For officialdom had arrived, customs officers had boarded the train, these money dealers were illegal.

They reached our carriage and were charming, names were exchanged, photos taken and prints promised, hands shaken and farewells said. I wish all custom men were so polite and helpful. Of course they were examining our luggage at the same time, no doubt a treat for them, our goods must have been interesting even if we were travelling light, compared to the monotony of African bundles.

For some reason after this, when we had crossed the border, it was decided to move us. We expostulated and Simon waved our tickets about but this had little effect as there wasn't a 'D' carriage and our numbered berths were missing. We had grown attached to our quarters but we followed our luggage as it was grabbed and slung around the shoulders of some men we hoped were porters. Our new compartment was dirtier than ever so Simon insisted that someone came and cleaned it. To my surprise someone did, not that it made much difference but honour was satisfied.

I was sorry when night came, blacking out the wonderful African scene. We were in Tanzania now and between the lakes Malawi and Tanganika. When daylight came we descended onto the plains and once again saw the vast stretches of countryside and the wandering wildlife. How dull flying seemed compared with the excitements of this journey.

Morning came and coke is not my best awakener. I missed my early morning 'cuppa'. However I was willing to forego my normal routine when there was so much to see outside and inside the train.

It soon became apparent that something was very wrong with the train. Gradually it was slowing down and the not too pleasant smell we had begun to notice became stronger and stronger. Simon went to investigate.

"Its a disgrace," he said, "the luggage van is full of day old chicks and they're all dying, it's too hot and they've no water. I suppose the price is better in Tanzania."

"Why then," I asked "is the train not speeding up?"

"I'll find out," he replied, disappearing again.

He returned with the news that everyone on the train, as far as he could ascertain, was involved in the chick enterprise and a whip-round was being organized to persuade the driver to go faster. He wanted his cut in the deal. Disbelieving but realizing that this was not England I suggested that Simon added to the collection. "For the sake of the chicks," he said.

I agreed, not adding that Mother had no desire to languish along with dead chicks for any longer than was necessary. Not that I wasn't enjoying the journey, it was so bustling and colourful at the various stops with the excited children and the busy touts. In contrast were the long stretches of deserted countryside with the sight of an occasional village. The train had probably once been well maintained, this maintenance now seemed an alien concept, it could be, and probably had been, one of the world's great rail journeys.

The financial tactics with the driver having been successful we arrived in Dar at last. We were very late and because of Simon's speed as he raced out of the station I never knew the fate of the chicks. I was surprised at the magnificence of the cathedral like station but I think it was mainly closed to stop the population taking up residence there.

There were taxis here and to my surprise and pleasure I found we were going to take one. It had seats and if the doors were held on with string, I was not prepared to notice. It went and I was in Dar where I'd always wanted to be, to me it had a romantic sound. We were not there long enough for me to be too greatly disillusioned.

The only hotel was full up. It wasn't of course 'the only hotel', it was the only hotel in Simon's book. It looked cool, comfortable and clean, I badly needed a wash and was looking forward to some food. We rejoined our taxi, the taxi-driver had waited hopefully and we were now his property. Sammy knew plenty places - 'no problem', so we meekly allowed ourselves to be guided by him and were taken to a back street 'we-don't-go-there' sort of hotel.

After we'd mended the plumbing, fixed the shower curtain, tidied up and put bits of paper under wobbly furniture we were perfectly comfortable.

If cupboard doors don't fit properly and there is no television it is immaterial to a traveller too tired to care. There was water and a fish supper, by a pool uninhabited by crocodiles, was excellent.

Breakfast was fine too, I requested eggs and these were not swimming in fat. The toast was freshly made, it was hot and there was marmalade.

Some white South Africans (this was before universal elections) demanded eggs and were told there weren't any. Is it the accent or the 'black bastard' approach I wonder? This last doesn't go down well.

We now tried to find the boat to take us to Mombasa. Sammy took us to the harbour and the boat was there, also was a notice telling of its magnificence and where and how to book a passage. The 'Virgin Butterfly' looked every bit as good as the advertisement suggested. The poster said it sailed from Mombasa to Dar but here it was in Dar so, of course I told myself, it had to return.

We went to the booking office.

"Yes, it might sail," we were told by a disinterested clerk.

"When?" we asked.

The replies were vague, the African usually likes to oblige.

"If enough people wish to go on it" didn't seem very hopeful.

We were short of time and Simon was getting fidgety, as we left the office one of the staff called us back.

"But it has engine trouble," he told us.

"Then it won't be going?"

"Not for some time," he replied, "Someone may mend it," he added cheerfully.

'Sometime' in African could mean anything.

"I suppose we'll have to fly," Simon said bringing me back to earth.

We never did get to Mombasa, we managed to book a flight to Nairobi leaving the following night, it was a return flight as Simon had been asked if he would mind driving a car back to Lusaka. He was delighted at the idea and knew, as always, of a good place to stop on this return journey through Tanzania.

Meanwhile Sammy took us around the town delighted that we had some more time with him. We found another hotel along the beach road, this road was bad even by African standards and recent rain had not improved it except to lay the worst of the dust. We had a choice of hotels and tossed up between no air conditioning, no water, and apparently no staff. We chose the one with water.

"We don't need air conditioning," I said foolishly, "We can always open the windows."

I was wrong, the mosquitos swarmed in and it was sometime before we managed to deal with them. I had grown to hate that ominous whining in the night.

The beach was lovely, perhaps these hotels too had once been first class to match their surroundings. We'd brought food with us and had a beach picnic, the small two flat cottages were arranged along the beach, the restaurant, bar and offices were in the centre. We went to the beautifully designed restaurant for breakfast, it was round, thatched and open on the beach side with views over the sea. We chose a table with this view in mind and wondered why all the other guests were in a huddle in a far corner. We were soon to learn. A nest of African bees hung within a few feet of us and we joined the other guests when we realized that no waiter would be so foolhardy as to wait on us. African bees are not to be trifled with, Simon pointed out that I had wanted to see wildlife and these were wild alright. I am allergic to bee stings and felt happier at a distance, I was not the only one.

That evening as we left this potentially perfect place we saw a bevy of air hostesses arriving, this short holiday on a wonderful Indian Ocean beach was probably part of their contracts but I did wonder if they preferred water to air-conditioning and if any of them had enough interest in entomology to enjoy breakfast with the bees.

It had seemed unadventurous to have to fly but I wasn't so sure when I saw the aircraft which was a modest plane of an unknown airline. Time and money had mattered more to Simon than knowledge of the airline, also it had no waiting list and so prompt a journey would allow us to have a few days in Nairobi in which to visit friends.

The old bus taxied across the runway but it was when we became airborne that I noticed that the seat belts were unattached.

"It doesn't really matter," said Simon, "because the seats are loose anyway."

By this time the cheerful air hostesses had come round with the sweets, perhaps to take our minds off trivialities, and cheaper than getting the seats fixed.

We flew over the top of Kilimanjaro and I felt Simon having one of his ideas - that of climbing this spectacular mountain. While his mind was thus engaged mine was hoping that our acquaintance with the mountain would not be a descent onto its vast snowy peaks.

We arrived safely.

"I'll change some money and then we'll find somewhere to stay," said Simon when we were through customs.

I didn't feel like 'finding somewhere' at 2 am, I felt like being there, so, with this in mind, I approached the stand of the most expensive hotel which advertised rooms, taxi awaiting, money changing, the lot.

"Don't bother!" I said firmly to Simon, dragging him from the queue he'd joined. "We're going here and the taxi is waiting for us."

For once he didn't argue.

The reception clerk at the hotel looked hard at us, he addressed me.

"Your son?" he asked.

I agreed to it.

"I'll book you in as mother and child," he informed us. Simon looked flabbergasted but as a true child it was financially an obvious advantage. It was late, no-one else was booking in.

Our time in Nairobi was to be brief.

"We shan't have time for all your friends," said Simon, but, as we stepped outside the hotel we came face to face with Paula. Her expression was something to remember, it was a combination of you-ought-to-be-in-England; who is this man. (She'd never met Simon) and amazed pleasure. All she said was, "Why didn't you let me know?"

"This is Simon," I said "and we didn't know ourselves."

"Of course you're staying," she said. "Joy knows where I live, I've room for you both. I've a meeting, see you later."

"I've a meeting too," said Simon, "I think I'd better hire a car."

I knew a back street garage where I though we might hire one inexpensively.

As we walked down Kenyatta Avenue I was accosted by the one-time cook on the Turkana trip.

"I've been waiting for you," he told me. He was an ugly man prepared to show me all his wounds and bruises. How many years was it? Waiting for me? What had I done to deserve this. He must be a very patient man. To Simon's disapproval I emptied my purse, there wasn't much in it.

"You do have some strange friends," said Simon.

We hired the car and Simon drove off in it. I found an outside cafe and watched the world go by. Nairobi is like that, it is said that everybody goes by, in time.

Simon was optimistic about our return journey.

"With any luck," he said, "that boat will have arrived in Mombasa by the time I've finished here so we can take the train to Mombasa and board it there."

We never did get to Mombasa. The 'Virgin Butterfly' was still sitting in the harbour at Dar when we returned there unenterprisingly by plane. We went to look at the bus but decided that the advice we had been given to avoid it was sound.

"If I'd been on my own . . ." said Simon thoughtfully. Well - perhaps - but I doubted it.

We had return tickets on the plane, it was a night flight and we were anxious to get going. Unexpected airport taxes had left us short of shillings and we needed some for the return journey, we were still far from home.

We were lucky in Dar because the car Simon was to take into Zambia had arrived at the port, big, brand-new and still in its wrapping paper, we were able to load ourselves into it and leave that morning. We had very little shopping to do, food for ourselves and as many toilet rolls as we could find (there was a shortage in Northern Zambia) didn't take us long and we now drove through the beautiful countryside we had seen from the train but which now seemed so much nearer. These words 'beautiful countryside' seem a tame way to describe the vastness of the African scenery. It still fills me with awe and wonder, those great remote peaks and the great stretches of plains. It looks so uninhabited and inaccessible. I try to think domestically, are there peaceful farms there and quiet tribes where people are thinking of their crops and what to have for the next meal? I find I cannot think in this small way when faced with the great expanse of land, my mind is dominated by the greatness of it.

First in the coastal regions were many of my favourite tree - the Baobab. They have huge trunks and branches come out of the top giving the appearance of roots giving it the popular name of 'upside-down-tree'.

We stopped at the side of the road where a youth was selling pineapples. There were many of these roadside stalls with children waving beautiful specimens at us. At first we resisted the temptation but then began to think, "Why resist?" We filled every available space in the car. It smelt delicious.

We saw many animals including a small herd of elephants with babies feeding beside the road and quite undisturbed by traffic. Not that there was much traffic in spite of it being a good road. The hills were in front of us and, leaving the plains, we drove onto the plateau again, we met up with the railway line here but did not see a train.

It grew dark, very dark with that velvety blackness through which I am unable to see. What surprised me most about my son is that he always seems to know where he is. On a main road in the sunshine I, too, was sure of our whereabouts but now in pitch black, miles from anywhere, I was not so sure. We were looking for a rest house, "Not far from here," Simon assured me. Where was here? I could not see a thing. Yet we arrived, or Simon said we had arrived, a gate was opened and a vague wooden building loomed up before us. There were steps and a veranda appearing in the car lights. Simon turned these out and went up the steps with our only torch.

"No-one here," he called out, "I'll get the keys."

He disappeared into the gloom, where, I wondered, where are the keys? I waited and waited, it seemed like hours, I could see a glow down by the gate and could hear faint grunts. These could have been anything and to my fertile imagination became a pride of hungry lions. I stayed in the car.

At last Simon returned and with the torch the grunting was revealed as the night watchman, and the glow the embers of his fire.

"Where were you?" I asked Simon.

"I had to find the key," he explained kindly as to the simple minded.

I bit back my reply as we mounted the steps, found and lit candles and so discovered the interior of this delightful wooded bungalow. I hope it is still there and hasn't been undermined by ants. We had it to ourselves, we'd bought food in Dar and Simon cooked us a simple meal.

We were on our way again early in the morning.

We reached the border, it looked more complicated that the train procedures, there were two custom sheds, plus officials, one on either side of the border with large gates and lots of high fencing. Getting through looked as if it might take some time.

We had a lot of pineapples and didn't wish to part with them but they looked tempting and could well be a reason for a long hold-up.

"Have you the name of our train friend?" I asked Simon, this man had seemed so helpful. Simon put his hand in his pocket and triumphantly brought out the card.

"Do you know Mr ......," he asked.

The atmosphere changed, Mr ..... was found and everything went smoothly. Would he accept a pineapple? He, accepted it in the spirit it was given and after a few rides in the car backwards and forwards over the border we said 'Goodbye' to him once more and were on our way.

We and the pineapples were welcomed back, we had a small 'pineapple-and-what-was-it-like-on-the-Tanzam' party and as Simon did not wish to go to Lusaka enquired as to who would like to take the car on the next lap. I was sorry to say 'goodbye' to it. Harry wanted a go in it and thought of many things he ought to do in Lusaka.

"How will you get back?" someone asked.

"The Tanzam, of course," we all said.

"No, sounds a bit too basic for me," admitted Harry who liked his home comforts. A driver would be given the task of taking it south. No doubt he would fill it with all his family and friends, not one of whom would mind an unreliable return journey by train, bus or by hitching a lift.

Simon and I, encouraged by our friends, wondered if we should write to the authorities and try to get the facilities and timing improved on the Tanzam as the journey itself was unrivalled.

"Which authorities?" everyone asked.

I expect it is still much the same.

My time was up again and I must return home. The place was part of me and each time leave taking became more difficult.

"Next year," I say once more as I board the plane for home.

CHAPTER 12

Those happy years went so quickly, I worked and while working looked forward to this yearly pilgrimage. At that time of the year it was a dramatic place to live, the short rains brought sudden noisy storms with lightning flashing through black massed clouds. There would be heavy drenching downpours and brilliant rainbows. Then sudden peace with a calm blue cloudless sky and a warm sunny day.

My love of Zambia grew over the years, my coming was expected and welcomed by the community on the hill as well as by the more scattered expat families. I loved the moment we left the hard road and bumped onto the red dirt maze where all knew us and came out to wave. Often the chief too would be there to add to the welcome.

The years brought changes, coffee gave way to sunflowers, the garden flourished as Luke began to know his trade, Simon added bits to the house and tried to encourage the making of compost. This idea of separating things out never really caught on and endless tins and plastic found their way into his fine organic pits. The dogs grew and so did the children, these last had their own pets, rabbits and guinea pigs, the dogs always looking hopefully at the cages. If the cages were not properly shut the inmates, with their fat little bodies, disappeared without trace.

William was still with us and occasionally brought little William, his small son, with him hoping that he would learn good English but he was much too shy of me to attempt even one word. In spite of William's Bemba wife he still held the tribe in contempt. At one time of the year a juicy caterpillar emerges in great numbers, it feeds from a particular tree, the name of which I have forgotten. When this luscious titbit is seen all work is forgotten and there is a noisy rush to the trees. The caterpillar disappears fast as it is a great delicacy. Some are popped into the childrens' mouths, healthier than sweets, I suppose.

William brought me one expecting a disgusted reaction.

"They eat these," he said.

"Why not if they enjoy them?" I replied, for who am I to criticise. In my own culture there are great delicacies that I would not touch such as certain shellfish, eaten raw, that are supposed to be the height of civilized eating.

Rose and Luke were now enjoying an unchallenged feast with much laughter and taunting of William for his non-participation. He retired in disgust to his kitchen. Later, in the market, I saw piles of these caterpillars (dead), perhaps they were nice fried?

Jennie gave up her small nursery group and went to teach part time at Elizabeth and Adam's school. Sometimes Peter went with her, sometimes he stayed with Rose, when I arrived and wanted to go with Simon to visit the farms I was able to take him with me. Some of these farms were a day's distance away and Simon had set up his own camp on the outskirts of a village, he could then stay there if he was working late. So when he said, "I'll be away two nights, you can come if you like," it was invitation enough for me!

"We'll take another tent," he said, "All you'll need will be your little camp bed, a sleeping bag and your mosquito net. We could build you another hut if you prefer." Just like that - my own hut! I declined the new hut, preferring my tent, I'm not sure I trust huts, the sides and roof are made of things that rustle, wonderful hiding places for things that "go bump in the night". Snakes may not go bump but my imagination suggests all sorts of goings on in the vegetation that surrounds me. In a tent, safely zipped in, I feel secure, there may not be much air but also there are no little gaps for intruders.

"We'll take Maggie," he said, "She can look after you."

I am not sure what this 'looking after' entailed but it was good to have Maggie, we had made friends at the office party, it was she who organized the dancing and tried to teach me how to waggle my hips.

I loved the camp, it was great for many from the village were employed by Simon's project and in the evening the men collected there for beer drinking, it was like the local pub. The fire would be banked up, the beer would be handed round. I avoided it, there was only one vessel and one straw.

The camp consisted of a central building with a thatched roof on pillars, this was Simon's office and had a table and canvas director chairs, there was a kitchen-store and a great pile of wood, also Simon's own sleeping hut. After seeing to the erection of my tent I looked around for the 'facilities'.

"Where," I asked Simon, "is the loo?" he showed me the pit, dug between camp and bush which, with a single waist-high wall, had so far served him adequately.

I viewed it with disfavour, I am not keen on crouching over pits, my ideas of simple basic living disappear when faced with reality. Simon now began to look at it with different eyes, he'd probably only used it in the dark and he set some men to build up the wall. A roof I didn't ask for, that would have been a luxury and I had brought an umbrella.

Someone was sent to look for a box and with much giggling and chattering a well shaped hole cut in the top, the chattering probably a discussion on the necessary size. It was placed over the hole and my approval sought. I went to look at this symbol of civilization and found that the wall did not extend to the bush side and several children from the village had gathered to watch the entertainment.

"Mother wants the wall this side as well," Simon explained to the men. To me he said, "You are fussy." However he returned to the men who were building the wall from the outside.

"Don't forget a way in," he said cheerfully, and to me, "Better than climbing over it."

He did know Africa.

Maggie considered serving my early morning tea to be part of looking after me. In the African dawn the wonderful brew she brought after blowing up the charcoal and adding to the tea some local grown lime and a taste of Zambian honey, was nectar indeed. No tea bag and bottled milk can ever be the same. Perhaps the charcoal is an additional bonus. I was never quite sure what Maggie did as Simon had described her as 'the office girl'. We corresponded for many years but, as every letter is in different handwriting and quite different style, I wondered, and still do, about her literacy.

Simon had described her as the office girl and when asked about her duties he had replied, "Oh! This and that," in an offhanded way. General comforts perhaps, or so I thought as quietly and smilingly she would bring a large tin mug with my tea and no-one else would wake.

Out here in the bush I was able to see something of the farming methods. I was fascinated by the Bemba system of shifting cultivation called 'Chitimene'. It is a rotational system suited to the soil which is poor in nutrients. A wide area is cleared and the vegetation including shrubs and trees are brought into a circle of cultivated ground, this is burnt and the circle of ground used for a rotation of various grains, maize and beans. I suppose this method was a bit like the old slash and burn which was practised when there was plenty of land and far fewer people. Here in Zambia there was room for the patch to be abandoned after three or four years and a new one started. Some of these circles were now some way away from the village while the near ones were regrowing. There was a plot quite near the camp but others required a long trek through the bush to reach them. I enjoyed these walks and found myself more at home in the bush than I had ever been.

Simon expressed fears that this Chitimene might die out as the older men died and the young men, uninterested in the skills needed, left for the towns.

One afternoon I was quietly drinking tea under the central roof shelter when a car went by, this in itself was an event but as I heard brakes I realized we had visitors. The car backed up and a disbelieving white man and his teenage son stared out. I wished I had cucumber sandwiches to offer them but they accepted tea with gratitude and when they drove off still had a look of incredulity. An explanation of 'Mother' didn't seem to satisfy them; I never asked what they were doing there, I don't think the track went anywhere.

On my very last visit Simon was there to meet me in Lusaka. The last visit because Simon's contract ended that summer, the family would be coming home, possibly for a year.

"Come and see," said Simon leading me to the airport car park and proudly presenting a brand new Land Rover. He had taken delivery of this for the project and it had everything, every possible gadget that Simon's heart could desire. Except papers.

"While I'm sorting things out and getting these why don't you get Mark to take you to Munga Wanga? I'd heard of these zoological gardens and in particular the famous Arboretum there.

Mark brightened considerably, he was driving a truck, much less dashing than the new vehicle, and obviously wasn't going to be allowed to get his hands on it.

"I ought to try it out," said Simon, "You've never been to the Victoria Falls have you? You ought to see them before we finish here. We could drive down to Livingstone and there's a reasonable camp near the falls."

I could hardly believe my luck. Amanda's daughter and my grand-daughter, Victoria, had made be promise to visit 'her' falls and here at last was the opportunity.

After I'd had a wash and brush up Mark and I drove off to Munga Wanga in the truck. He was strangely jaunty.

"I hear there's a lion there," he said.

We were in Africa so I turned to him in some amazement.

"Have you never seen a lion?" I Asked.

"No," he said wistfully, "And I want to see this animal."

Of course he should see his lion but I thought it would probably be a mangy specimen compared to some of those I had seen in the wild. Probably in England we had better specimens in wildlife parks.

I was right, I wasn't terribly impressed with the zoo, the enclosures were too small, this was Africa where animals roamed free. I felt dispirited, would it all eventually come to this. I was cheered though, while walking round one animal was free, a baby elephant joined me, decided I was his Mum and trailed endearingly behind me. In spite of notices saying 'Animals must not be fed, teased or poked' he may have been expecting a treat. I said 'Good Morning' to him in the politest way and left for the arboretum. I also left Mark gazing with delight at his lion.

The gardens, and particularly the trees, were lovely, most of the names meant nothing to me so I decided to enjoy the place for its own sake, it was peaceful here too after the hurly burly of Lusaka. A notice said 'Do Not carve on the plants'. I had not brought my carving knife and I did wonder who would want to carve on these beautiful trees.

After a time I left this secluded and tranquil place and went in search of Mark. I found him with a group of friends in a cafe area. Simon had given me some Kwacha for the entrance fee and anything else we needed, I called Mark over and slipped him some, with ten children he probably didn't have much pocket money. I waited for him to rejoin his friends to save him the embarrassment of having to sit with me. I retreated to the gardens.

We drove back to town and met up again with Simon.

"Are we staying here?" I now asked, I was suffering with jet lag and was unsure of the time.

"No, we'll drive straight down, camp there tonight and visit the falls tomorrow."

He gave last minute instructions to Mark who was returning, and we were off.

We had gone some miles before he announced, "I haven't got the papers yet, so we can't drive over the border."

"Does it matter?" I asked, not having a great idea of the geography of that area.

"Not a bit," he said cheerfully, "because we can walk."

It started to rain and then it grew dark, it wasn't like rain, it was like water tipping out of the skies. For all I knew we were already under the falls. There was nothing but water and blackness but Simon drove on, assuring me brightly every now and again that there was nothing to worry about. I had to take his word for it and, as he seemed perfectly happy, I assumed the Land Rover was going well. We were snug and water-tight, I relaxed.

We arrived at the camp and the huts were in the middle of nowhere they didn't look as water-tight as the Land Rover. Simon was still cheerful and disappeared into the night saying, "No-one will come out in this so I'd better book us in and get some keys."

He reappeared jangling these, fitted them into the locks of two adjoining huts and, most important of all, fitted the Land Rover neatly in the convenient exact-sized space between them.

My hut was clean and holes in a mosquito net no longer present problems to me, I have learnt to tie them up, my own net was far away at the bungalow where I seldom need it. When I do, I haven't got it.

We had supper at the restaurant, here there were plenty of staff and very few guests. The fish was excellent.

On waking I looked out and saw that monkeys had taken

possession of the precious vehicle. Horrified I hurried out to chase them away and I was hastily rubbing out their feet marks when Simon appeared. The rain had stopped and it promised to be a lovely day.

After breakfast we set off.

"It's not far," said Simon.

This should have been enough to put me on my guard but we had been walking for some time before it struck me that we didn't seem to be getting anywhere.

"How far is it?" I asked, for I found it frustrating to hear the thundering of the waters but still not to see anything.

"We cross that bridge just over there," he replied, bracingly.

In the far distance I admitted I could see a white bridge.

"It goes right over a gorge, we walk over it, you'll love it," Simon urged me on.

It looked miles away but it was a fine morning and where was my pioneering spirit? No doubt Livingstone himself had heard the noise and hurried to see this wonder. We arrived at last and my ambition was completely fulfilled.

There are plenty of good guide books about the Victoria Falls or Mosi-oa-Tunya (translated 'the smoke that thunders') as they were, it seems, called by the Kololo people, this thunder can be heard from a long way off. None of the books, nor I, can do justice to the magnificence of the scene, nothing prepares you for the theatrical beauty of this exciting and spectacular place. I felt like stout Cortez as I stood viewing these wondrous rushing waters.

The wide Zambesi flows peacefully along around small green islands and then it meets this drop, no wonder it thunders and sends up smoke like spray, the contrast is dramatic, over thousands of years the river has retreated as the rock wears away and this has formed the narrow, zigzag gorges where a now wild river races. There was white water rafting here, I didn't think I'd bother.

So I was seeing the Zambesi at last and I was happy. One book I read said that the falls should be seen at all seasons and at all times of day and night, it was mid-December and the main rain from up country had not yet reached here. It must be even more sensational then, as it was I was satisfied and I thought it unlikely I should ever return again.

I preferred the Zambian side, any touristy bits were well away from the fall, it seemed more natural, some attempt had been made at one time to put up coloured lights but fortunately these no longer worked. The Zimbabwe side is more popular, with a hotel and many people. There was a school party and, remembering my own well organized and carefully watched over groups back home, I was worried when some of these children lent over the side and threw down stones.

"It's not your business," said Simon. I refrained from comment but thought it was everybody's business, even if on holiday, to stop a child falling to its doom.

The constant spray falling on vegetation has created a rain forest and we wandered through this and were thoroughly drenched. We soon dried out over lunch in the Victoria Falls hotel where a band played, it was an excellent band, the best African band I'd heard. A pity it wasn't somewhere else.

Before returning to Zambia we decided to visit the town of Victoria Falls. There was a train waiting at the station, it had Rhodesian Railways still written on it. I had forgotten that I was in the old Rhodesia and I again remembered my tattered history book, my atlas and my classroom reveries.

"Better just look in the shops," said Simon, having changed money in the hotel.

"Soon be Christmas," I agreed.

Shopping proved more attractive than we had anticipated, we seemed to have rather a lot of odd shaped parcels.

"I'd better find a taxi," said Simon. "You wait here."

Everywhere I've been there have always been plenty of taxis, some falling to bits I'd admit but still providing their owners with a moderate living. Here in Zimbabwe it seemed an unknown concept.

"We'll have to walk," said Simon, returning empty handed, or wheel-less I should say, and, hung around with our various purchases we set off for Zambia. What a good job I didn't buy that large rug and the full sized carved statue. That will teach me to go shopping, I thought, I was hot and tired and although Simon shouldered most of the bundles, some were his, I wasn't relishing the walk as we had some way to go, it had seemed a long way coming, now, in retreat, it seemed twice as far.

Crossing the border into Zimbabwe had presented no problems, now returning was a different story. At the border post there was a long queue of African foot travellers all carrying the extraordinary collection of bags and boxes that makes up African luggage. Mine was similar. It was hot and shadeless but inside the hut unwelcoming, hot and stuffy. A slow, very slow examination of every person and every bundle was taking place. I stayed outside and joined the queue Simon preferred inside hoping to see some method of easing our way. When it came it was from a different direction and unexpected.

Someone in Zimbabwe had found a taxi, because one came now, came fast and furiously with slamming of brakes in a dramatic fashion, there was a sudden commotion as a woman jumped out, desperation in her every movement. She rushed to the desk declaring an emergency with a tale of sickness and plane times. But money was required and she had none of the right currency. The officials were not to be flustered. They were adamant and unrelenting. Simon, one of those pushed aside by the woman's urgent aggression, saw the waiting taxi and his opportunity.

"How much does she need?" he asked.

She could have kissed him.

"I'll let you have the money if you'll take my Mother in your taxi."

Relief came to her and to me.

"I'll pay you back," she was saying as she and I were rushed through customs and Simon pushed me into the taxi and dumped all our bags on top of me.

"Don't worry," he said, "Taking Mother is all I want."

There was a small space though, and he squeezed in beside me. No-one complained. We arrived back at the camp, thanks and blessings still following us. The Land Rover was safely where we'd left it.

* * *

The Lusaka road we had travelled down on, seen by daylight and in fine weather, looked, on our return journey, innocent enough, so I was in a relaxed mood and dozing slightly as we drove along it. When the Land Rover came to an abrupt halt I was thinking more in terms of cups of tea than of any emergency. There was no traffic and nothing in sight, the perfect spot for a picnic.

"No petrol," said Simon briefly. Something came up behind us, he got out, hitched a lift and was gone. The perfect picnic place now looked like a desolate wilderness, all bush and nothing moving.

I consoled myself with the thought that he would be bound to return, nothing would part him from his beloved Land Rover. I remembered my thermos and patiently waited.

In Kenya my presence would have been soon discovered and from hidden villages people would have gathered, but not here. There was complete silence. A similar incident happened to me in Dorset when my grandson George, in a clapped out student car, failed to persuade it up a hill. He got out, "I'll walk to the nearest garage."

"I'll come too," I said.

"Sorry," he replied. "It doesn't lock, you'll have to stay with it." I hadn't a thermos, it was cold. Africa seemed, suddenly, very friendly and a long way off.

* * *

Simon still had his mind on his fishing trip to Lake Tanganyika so Christmas was a hurried affair that year. Nothing was missed out, the party, the singing and the happy collection of people, but our departure for the lake on Boxing Day was not greatly advertised and only a few of us made our way there.

Instead of the tented camp with monkeys and no lights we had the best huts and ate in the hotel. It was very civilized.

It was a beautiful wooded area, the huts were among trees and shrubs so that when I received a bite causing intense pain I should not have been surprised.

"It's only a tsetse fly," said Simon.

"Isn't this a free area?" I asked, fighting back the water that seemed to be streaming from my eyes. Everywhere we went we'd been sprayed.

"There aren't any cattle here so it doesn't matter. Don't worry," he added, "they don't carry malaria."

"What do they carry?" I was recovering but very cross.

"Sleeping sickness, that is if it's an infected fly."

"How soon shall I know?" the pain was fading.

"In about three weeks," he replied, and added with a bright smile, "You'll be home by then."

Thank goodness for Jennie, practical as always and sympathetic with it, had departed for the right ointment and now arrived with anthisan and pain killers.

I didn't develop the disease but I did look it up and now feel I am an authority on Trypanosomes, the protozoa that causes sleeping sickness.

The pain passed and this incident didn't spoil my enjoyment of the rest of this short holiday.

We ate fish caught by Simon and Adam, I went down to meet the boat and took a photo of Adam with a fish, larger than himself, that he insisted he had caught, I was doubtful but there were many grins among the men so I realized he was to be given the credit for it.

We didn't however eat the small fish called Kapenta that is caught in the lake here, dried and sent all over Zambia. I'd seen them piled high alongside the caterpillars in the market places. Simon asked me if I'd like to see the drying process and the smell of the place was pretty powerful even from a distance; we didn't stay long. One of the workers there, enquiring if I was returning to England, asked if I would take some to a friend of his who was studying there. I had to refuse.

Simon had, vaguely, the idea of permanency. While by the lake we went to see a farm he'd heard of that he thought might be for sale.

"Well not for sale exactly, more of a partnership?"

Jennie was dubious about the idea.

"We've the childrens' education to think about, where is it anyway?"

Simon was as optimistic as ever. "School things all come in the post!"

We all knew the post, it was hardly reliable.

"This chap wants to sell part of the farm, he wants someone to work with who knows the country and his wife wants company."

"So it's miles from anywhere?" asked Jennie, who never wants for company.

"Let's go and look at it." I suggested, "It's a jaunt anyway, and might give us ideas."

Jennie agreed and we all went visiting.

It turned out we'd all been asked to lunch so the visit had already been arranged.

I can see what people think when Mumma comes too, not for them the hard-working penny-pinching do-it-on-the-cheap traveller but the rich holding-the-purse strings parent who is going to dish out the lolly. It amuses me so I try to give good measure and play the part. Simon will play up too and neither Jennie or myself will let him do anything rash. It was a beautiful house with a wonderful view and while Simon was enthusing, Jennie and I were asking a few awkward questions. The beautiful house with the wonderful view was not for the sucker of a partner who was to live in an old Chinese built dwelling situated down on the plain in what looked to me very like a swamp. We walked round it, Simon reassuring us, with decreasing enthusiasm, as to its possibilities. We all knew it wouldn't do.

Perhaps the good lunch was meant to soften us, unfortunately the farmer was drunk most of the time, perhaps he realized that as buyers we were unlikely candidates. Mumma was a dead loss.

"If," said Jennie as we drove back to the lake. "If it were a nice house (with a swimming pool added Elizabeth) and a lovely view, if it were cheap and there was a good school ..."

I saw the letter Simon wrote, stating his requirements for his side of the deal and what he expected to get out of it. Even if the farmer wasn't sober when he received it, I feel sure he would be after he read it. We didn't hear again.

By the time we were back home Simon's interest in the idea of his own African farm had waned, the childrens' education had begun to become an important issue if they weren't to be sent to boarding school.

"What's the good of having children if you send them away?" said Simon, so short term contracts and living at home would have to be the answer.

"If you're away you won't see them anyway," I pointed out but he dismissed this as irrelevant.

Tales of the crocodile farm had reached the children and they all wanted to go and see it as it was only a short boat ride away so we visited it before we left the lake. It was another remarkably smelly place, I am not fond of crocodiles and even seeing babies just hatched from their eggs did nothing to endear them to me, the enormous hungry looking just-ready-for-Italian-shoes-and-handbags were quite frightening even from behind their fences. I could never wear croc shoes even if they were suitable to my muddy existence, I'd always remember the smell.

Another short boat trip away were some hot springs, this sounded interesting.

"Only a short walk," the boatman assured us. I had forgotten that 'short walk' in Africa can mean almost anything. We boated up the coast and then walked and walked, the children began to complain, the grass and reeds through which we walked were too high to see where we were going, the narrow path meandered around, avoiding various little bogs. We reached the springs at last, they were not spectacular, I'd imagined them like those I'd seen at Lake Bogoria in Kenya, we looked and returned to the boat, we were tired and hot and Peter needed a piggy-back. It seemed strange to be walking through African bush in this nonchalant way.

Our lakeside break over I was watching from my bedroom window as Simon packed up to visit his farms.

"How long will you be away?" I asked.

"Only two or three days, come if you like," he replied. The children were with him watching and listening.

"Can I come?" asked Lizzie.

"Can I come?" asked Adam.

Peter wasted no words but came inside to fetch his Teddy bear. I went outside and Jennie joined me looking unusually cheerful.

"If you're looking after them," said Simon to me, "It's okay by me."

I turned to Jennie.

"I'll have a few days here," she said firmly.

She helped us to gather our things, the pile grew, the sleeping bags, my bed, extra food and washing things.

"Why washing things?" said Lizzie scornfully. "We don't have to wash surely?"

"You have to clean your teeth."

Lizzie signed deeply at the trivial minds of grown-ups. Adam fetched his bike, Peter fetched his football, Simon sent away for Maggie and another truck.

We were a sensation when we arrived, we were only to be away for two or three days before term started but this looked like the real thing, in my imagination I could see it, at last, as a real old time safari, people collected around us, Maggie took charge of the kitchen, tents went up, everyone helped with the unpacking, chairs came out, the bike was admired. How the villagers loved it. None of those early travellers had three children and a football, the football alone drew a small crowd, Adam and Peter had a following all their own. When night came one small boy stayed, no way was he going to lose sight of that ball.

"Is it all right?" I asked Simon. "Won't someone miss him?"

"I doubt it," said Simon. "They'll know where he is." The bush telegraph.

Washing suddenly became an absolute necessity to the children when they saw Simon's latest mod-con. We now had a shower, this consisted of a large oil drum supported on a platform with a simple pulling devise that worked most satisfactorily. Showers were best in the evening when the sun had warmed the drum.

The boy attachment, Eliot, went everywhere with us, carrying Peter if he complained but was first on the roof of the Land Rover when, at one village, the call of 'rabies' was heard. We all moved fairly fast, climbing back in and slamming the doors. A mad dog was loose, it was chased off and no-one in our party volunteered to go and verify the diagnosis.

Lizzie's scorn of washing was forgotten too when during some very hot walks we came across bubbling streams, in they plunged while I thought of all the horrible creatures that are supposed to inhabit African waters. Eliot, too, merely watched their antics.

Adam, riding his bike up and down the dirt road alongside the camp attracted quite a bit of notice. I was in the camp when I heard great laughter and went out to investigate. Adam had hit a stone and fallen off his bicycle, no-one went to see if he was hurt although the bicycle was on top of him, blood was pouring down his leg and tears down his face. I comforted him and took him and the bicycle into camp for repairs. I like to think that these women were laughing because they thought he was performing some trick for their amusement but I am not sure.

A small green snake, slithering through the camp, caused great excitement. There was shouting and rushing about and stone throwing, it hid in the woodpile which had to be demolished and more people joined the hunt. I tried to keep the children away but the excitement of battle spread to them too. I ran for my camera.

"A green mamba," one of the men told me, it wasn't very big but I was told it was deadly. I took the photo but, very dead, it wasn't impressive.

The fire would be lit in the evening and supper eaten sitting round it, bedtime was no problem, the children could see the glowing fire and soon fell asleep. On our last night after putting them to bed I joined the men around the fire, it was an occasion, for the chief was coming.

"Should I give him a present?" I asked Simon.

"What have you got?" he wanted to know.

I thought hard, I had nothing suitable with me - unless ...

"Would my umbrella do?"

"Excellent," said Simon.

It was one of those short ones that springs open.

The Chief came, beer went round and he made a speech. He spoke no English and it went on a long time, emphasised with much hand clapping.

"What did he say," I asked one of the men who spoke English.

"He says you son is a good man," he replied. I waited for the rest but that seemed to be it, there must be a great many Bemba words to one English and why the smiles, nods and laughter. The speech continued, his interpreter now said, "He has done much for the village and he will let Kenneth Kaunda know."

How? I wondered.

I fetched the umbrella and made the presentation, the Chief loved it, it was a very pretty one with pink roses.

Another long speech followed obviously of thanks. I turned to the interpreter.

"He can't wait for it to rain." Everyone laughed but the Chief looked worried, I don't think what he'd said was meant to be funny.

Next day we packed up and departed, Adam and Peter had a short debate and made their own presentation. Eliot received the football and clutched it to his chest, I expect he slept with his head on it.

A few days more to say 'Goodbye' to all my friends and the country. The family would be returning home soon so that was not so bad but it seemed unlikely that I should ever return to Zambia.

Mark drove me to Lusaka and the night flight, we saw Kenneth Kaunda at the airport, perhaps I should have brought the Chief's letter with me but I doubt if it was ever written.

CHAPTER 13

"Are you doing anything?" asked Simon nonchalantly. It was raining hard, Jennie was at work and I visualized a car stuck somewhere that needed a push.

"In what way?" I ask cautiously, "I'm busy at the moment." To myself I justify this because there is as always much to be done even if I'm not doing it.

"I mean long term," he replied, "I wondered if you'd like to come to Pakistan?"

Pause, while I think of all the things I'm not doing and mentally apologize for thinking of my son as a perpetually in-trouble teenager. I also take a quick mental look into the coffers and I am ready with my reply. Did he ever have any doubts of it, I wonder?

"When are we going?" I ask.

"As soon as you've sorted out your Visas," he says in his official voice. "Jennie can't come this time and I need someone of my tribe around. I assure you it'll be five star hotels all the way."

I am doubtful, not about the trip but about the hotels. Five star? No plumbing problems, no non-working lifts, none of 'we-don't-go-there' sort of places. How very dull it sounds, but I soon cheer up because I am sure it won't be like that. After all it never is.

"I may have to go to India too," Simon adds as an extra incentive. "We could fix that elephant ride you've always hankered after."

I am already visualizing next year's Christmas card, no holly, robins or mistletoe, just me on an elephant.

Alas it is not only visas I need. My passport, now a well-worn worthy document, is out of date, I have to part with this big blue one, which now consists of two stapled together by the Nigerian High Commission, and accept an inferior red European one. Its the first time I've resented Europe, my old falling-apart book meant something to me.

I start having new photos taken. I always blame the camera booths for these proofs of my increasing age. I realize I am deteriorating fast and do not need reminding of it. I look back at the last lot and think how young I looked, no doubt in a few years I shall look back at these and think the same.

My next step was to find some guide books. I was greatly cheered on reading Isobel Shaw's 'Pakistan Handbook' to hear that, "To the spirit hungry for exploration and adventure - Pakistan calls." For a moment this halted my thinking and to myself I said "Pakistan here I come, Mother is on her way."

This time I assured myself I shall make extensive notes all the time, I shall not, as I have done so far, write on scrappy bits of paper in an incomprehensible scrawl. This time I shall go prepared as real travelling writers do and write up all my thoughts and doings methodically from day to day.

Now, today, as I try to sort through all these scrappy scribbles, I remember this resolution with regret. However there is always a next time.

"Can you be ready by Thursday?" asks Simon one Monday morning as if it was a shopping trip. "Don't worry, I've got the tickets." So I didn't have a choice.

Luckily all my documents had come through and probably my wardrobe had enough suitable garments for an Islamic country. Long skirts were 'in' anyway. I am not given to very short shorts or very revealing blouses.

Medically I was inadequately informed and protected. I was still within my yellow fever inoculation period, but what else should I need?

"Nothing else," said Simon, "There's no malaria at this time of year," he pauses "Perhaps you had better take something for Pakistan Tummy." I did not wish to return to the doctor. He had given me a 'flu jab because it was said to be a vicious Asian variety. I was quite chuffed to think this was something I wouldn't get in Asia. On the other hand I felt quite ill after it and did not want to add to my troubles. I tell myself I must trust Simon, after all he knows best, so I risk it.

Amanda generally comes to help when she thinks I am 'off' somewhere. This gives her satisfaction as she can reassure herself that all is running smoothly and Tom is okay. While he waits, hopefully, for her to go away I fall over her boots left in the middle of the sitting room, remove dog biscuits from my luggage and, instead of thinking constructively, am distracted by inappropriate articles left about and every domestic utensil being in the wrong place.

We were off at last and I wondered if those great women travellers with all their gear felt butterflies in their insides as I do. They went into the unknown and I am going with my son to five star treatment. Or am I? For me it's the time before I am on the move, once going I am fine, perhaps they were the same.

Pakistan seems to be all men. We were met by Simon's driver and driven to - yes - a five star hotel. I didn't know it at the time but it was the last five star hotel on the trip.

I was tired and, in spite of getting off the plan among the first rush and Simon dragging me at full speed to the luggage conveyor belt, ours was about the last to emerge. It was now 4 am and my room was everything I could wish for. An enormous bed, fruit, flowers, television and, thankfully, phone with which to order anything I wished. I was too tired to appreciate the finer points. I ordered tea and immediately found fault, I decided it was buffalo milk. I rang Simon to complain.

"It's your imagination, go to sleep. You don't need tea this time of the night anyway."

What time of the night is it? I thought hard but jet lag won and I fell asleep.

When I awoke I heard someone at the door, I thought it must be Simon and opened the door to a beautiful young man with more roses, this was a new experience, one which my hardy travelling ladies never encountered. It was now 12 noon but only 7 am to me.

We were to stay another day in Karachi and I remembered the warnings of my family who had visited last year. They all said, "You'll never believe the awfulness of the traffic?" "It's smoky and smelly too," said Elizabeth, now well into environmental problems.

"I know all about traffic," I told her in a superior way, "I have been in Nigeria you know."

"It's worse than that," she said.

I didn't know, nothing really prepared me for the chaos, fumes and noise of Pakistan and India. The noise because every driver seems to believe that by putting his hand on the horn, Klaxon or hooter, all trouble will be avoided. Their faith must be strong for their observance of traffic laws is weak. In between all the cars, auto-rickshaws, buses and lorries are bicycles, camels, donkeys and horses. If I'd been given to headaches I should have had a bad one but fortunately I saw a beautifully decorated horse and carriage and, after a refreshing cup of tea, Simon accompanied me on a tour of the town. In this vehicle, known as a Victoria, we also weaved our way through the traffic. I admired the calm stability of the horse and driver, it seemed that as steam gives way to sail, so motor vehicles give way to animals.

Simon was pleased that my mind was so taken up with the horse that I was forgetting the noise, it was a touristy but delightful manner to progress and visit the sights.

In the middle of a road we came across a large green marquee.

"What's going on?" I asked Simon.

"It's the wedding season," he replied, "That's for the reception, we'll see weddings everywhere." We did, and I tried to imagine what would happen if a wedding reception was held in a tent in the middle of the road in Britain. On the M5 perhaps.

"The weddings have to be over by Ramazan," explained Simon.

We did meet weddings and the trappings everywhere, not only the festivities which must have cost a fortune, but garlands of roses everywhere. Simon bought one to hang round my neck, I later dried the petals and have them still.

"There's a swimming pool in the hotel," said Simon. It sounded inviting, it was a warm evening. It was not to be, the pool was full of Balloons as there was another wedding reception, the pool was roped off but as Pakistan is a dry country it was unlikely that the guests would end up in it.

By dry I mean nonalcoholic. Just as well with the traffic, at least the drivers were sober.

My first impression was of the noise and this included the calls to prayer. These raucous sounds came from loudspeakers and clashed with each other, gone was my romantic concept of saintly calls to the faithful from Minarets. Other impressions were the fantastically painted vehicles, everyone vied with everyone else and not an inch is left uncoloured. I feel this is environmentally friendly and not injurious to anyone else's health or eardrums. Beauty, too, in the garlands of roses and in the artistic arrangements of the fruit and vegetable stalls. It is as well to look for beauty when so much is filthy, where spitting seems to be the norm and beggars lie in wait for the unwary. I am not unsympathetic and find this very distressing. I found in Africa that it was best to choose one and ignore the others. Simon does the same. I force myself to think it is surely a government problem and not mine.

Next day we travelled north to Simon's project and the guest house, this had a gentle flowery name and I had pictured a small cosy establishment so I was not prepared for spacious lose-yourself-in-the-corridors marble. There were many men servants, all of whom had names beginning with A, I thought I would never master them and I never did. There was a cook, a bearer, two chokidars and a mali. Simon said I could do what I liked in the kitchen but beyond checking that the water was boiled and filtered I decided that kitchens and I could well afford a break. I could see Simon's point though and, after trying some of the cook's peculiar dishes, I stuck largely to eggs, bringing forth the remark, "Mother does like her eggs!" This liking was more for the care of my inside than any particular partiality for eggs. They seemed safe while some of the things Simon tackled, even though he enjoys Pakistani food, looked distinctly doubtful.

The job of the bearer was to keep the house clean, there was an impressive list of his duties hanging on the kitchen wall, I wondered if he had ever read it but he sang well and you can't have everything. The chokidars are the guards, one was on duty during the day and one at night. The daytime one seemed bored to death but we had many conversations and he picked me endless bunches of flowers. I never enquired as to the source of these bouquets. The mali also brought flowers otherwise his duties were never explained to me. But who am I to complain about domestic servants?

I have a vision of Mrs R, who comes in to oblige, if I'm lucky, one morning a week and a hurriedly dismissed vision of my ex-gardener who, in one short afternoon broke the fork, a rake and a very expensive wheelbarrow. So two softspoken, quiet men who don't seem over worried about the dusting seem like a gift from heaven. I wondered if Tom would have thought of the dusting, or, for that matter, the washing up which may be piled up in the sink awaiting my return. One thing is certain, he will have told Mrs R that she is not needed when I'm not there, convinced as he is that he is no trouble to anyone.

I was in a hurry on our arrival, Pakistani Tummy had already hit me, I was glad to find my room and 'facilities'. My running was noticed by Simon who, when I said, "It must have been the hotel," was visibly cheered and, rather callously I thought, said, "Oh good, we don't need to go to any more five star hotels then, there are plenty much cheaper and just as good - well nearly as good if you know where to look."

I knew he would know or would soon find out and, although there would be no more handsome men with roses, I should be just as comfortable, find plenty to enjoy and probably be more relaxed.

Before we travelled again I had a brief idyllic lull in the guest house. During this time I enjoyed a wide veranda and made friends with two or three delightful squirrels and many birds. These last I was unable to identify but I did recognize a Hoopoo with its long probing beak.

A mysterious set of stairs led up to a locked door and I found a key that fitted among the many hanging in the kitchen. I had a new domain then, as a flat roof overlooking the countryside was revealed. I could see the endless games of cricket, a polo ground, identify the various cries and calls from men and children selling things from hand-barrows and follow the progress of the goats herded by children whose schooling seemed to be non-existent.

We went shopping in the evening, the liveliest time. We bought fruit in plenty from the attractive stalls and many other necessities such as the vegetable extract to which Simon is addicted and some condensed milk for my early morning tea. The milk is always boiled for the tea, endlessly served all over the country, it tastes odd but it's safe. The tinned milk was not perfection but I knew the name on the tin.

The town here was, if anything, worse than Karachi, it is as environmentally unfriendly as it could possibly be, it seemed to be in a haze of dust and fumes.

The shops in the towns tend to be in groups according to their merchandise, for instance all the shoe shops are near to each other and materials shops in another cluster. This makes shopping for a certain commodity easy as you don't have to wander all over town. I loved the materials and bought several pieces with the idea of visiting 'Quickladiestaylor' which was only five minutes walk from the guest house. I'd seen this establishment in passing and wondered if my plain garments could be copied.

The bearer brought my breakfast to the veranda with the local newspaper. In this paper I read an article by an American who had visited the country briefly and whose rose coloured spectacle account added that he hadn't seen a single camel in this progressive country. Poor fellow, where had he been not to have seen these magnificent beasts? I saw them everywhere, here was true Eastern Romance for a camel train is a sight never to be forgotten. They sail along on their great flat feet, heads in the air, seeming to wear disdainful expressions and pulling huge loads. Their movement is in great contrast to the trot trot of the little donkeys.

The wildlife here differed considerably from that I had seen in Africa. On my third day I saw a ginger kitten on the ramparts, or what would have been the ramparts if this had been a castle. I was a little worried for the birds and the attractive striped squirrels and was doubtful about the introduction of a cat family. This small member saw me and started squeaking with a 'fetch-the-fire-brigade - I-can't-get-down' squeak. I thought the chances of the fire brigade even with a fire were remote and for a cat - well, not a hope. It had got up there I told myself, so logically it could get down and it had an excellent route with good tree branches. It eventually joined me on the terrace and made no move to chase other life. Bringing it bits of food though brought me to the notice of other feline prowlers and by the end of the week I had a beautiful pregnant and starved looking tortoise shell and a fine but equally hungry tabby tom. In the distance a black and white observed us with distrustful eyes.

A nice little frog appeared in my shower room and, as the door fitted reasonably well, I surmised that it had arrived by way of the plumbing. It came and went and I had to be careful not to step on it if I needed to visit the loo in the night. I also had to be careful not to leave the shower room door open or it might never have returned to its subterranean passages. I mentioned my visitor to Simon.

"Oh yes, Freddie," he said, "If he's there snakes won't be, otherwise he'd be eaten."

I'd never have thought of that, so I was right to encourage Freddie. I had only thought of him as a mosquito eater.

This peaceful interlude was interrupted when Simon said, "I have to go to Sukkar, you should come as you ought to see the barrage."

I admit I ought to see the barrage, especially as it seems to occur frequently in conversation but I also had to admit, and this to myself, that I was very vague about its purpose. This was soon remedied by consulting my guide books. A barrage is a dam, it creates head waters and the irrigation system is developed from this; the Sukkar barrage was the first to be built in Sind and consists of seven canals taking water across the plains from the River Indus.

So to Sukkar we went although my mind was not so much on recent Indian engineering works as on old civilizations and I wanted to visit Moenjodaro. This remarkable place had been the subject of a television programme which greatly impressed me. Simon was cheerful, "Don't worry, we'll fit it in on this trip, I'd quite like to go there myself."

My grandson, George, now studying archaeology, had been insistent that I visited the site so it was a promise to him as well as to myself. I was to bring back information and any interesting finds.

PIA, the Pakistan airline, operates remarkable good internal flights. We took one now.

The airports are modern and the officials pleasant, the searches are necessary but the girls are helpful and interested, sometimes too interested, in my possessions. If I lost all my batteries every time it was my fault, there was a system of retrieval at the other end but we never thought it worth the trouble to collect. We must have been good for the battery industry.

We arrived at the hotel in a yellow cab. There are always plenty of these, Simon has a system of 'go-to-the-first-on-the-rank' for fairness but I like to be sure of an English speaking driver as it saves a good deal of trouble.

"You'll like this hotel," said Simon, "I'll see if I can get you my old room."

He could, and he presented it proudly as his own creation. I could see why he liked it, the room was spacious and lofty, quite different from the characterless uniformity of the modern hotel. The furniture was a delight in itself being made of painted wood, all straight pieces so that it had a square look.

"It's made at a place called Hala," Simon informed me, "We'll go there one free day. There may be a few things you'd like to buy," he added, hopefully I thought, as this generally means that there are a few things he would like to buy. I let the remark pass and agreed that it might be a useful place to look for presents.

I don't know how may stars should be allotted for the entertainment that now followed. There were endless comings and goings, men bringing tea, filling the water container, mending the cistern and the television and finally to bring candles in case the electricity failed. I was also presented with a menu from which I could choose some interesting dishes. These included a 'sadwich', 'deeps fried fish', 'a speciality from the soil lovingly marinated', 'bonless chicken', 'a salad topped with boiled egg cuts', and for afters 'jelly three in one' or 'fruit triffle'.

After this, as Simon went off, I rested on the magnificent bed and fell instantly asleep to awake at 4 pm. After a time I managed to get the phone to work and ordered tea. It was getting chilly and I asked for a fire, it was brought by a very young man who, finding the plug didn't fit, removed it and pushed the wires into the socket! Prayer can be a useful thing.

Simon now returned and we decided to have an evening meal in the dining room. We met an acquaintance of Simon's at the reception desk. I felt that this Steve would have been propping up the bar in any other country.

"Mother wants to see Moenjodaro," Simon told him, "Is it worth a visit?"

"Not worth bothering with, old boy," replied Steve, "Just nip round to say you've been there."

I felt disheartened at this.

"Don't worry," said Simon, "He's always like that, I've booked tickets for the flight tomorrow anyway. We're going."

There is an airport at Moenjodaro and, although the guide book said, 'Take your own food' this was unnecessary as we were given a packed lunch as we left the aircraft. According to my appetite there was nearly a week's food supply but it proved useful at the site for, although the cafe served tea the facilities for food were minus stars rather than plus.

The ancient site was fantastic, how could anybody say 'Don't bother'? "Chacun à son gout," said Simon as we agreed that we would not, for anything, have missed the experience. It is as well not to accept other people's opinions.

We had a feeling as we wandered round that life was still going on as it was over 4000 years ago, the city had a feeling of only yesterday, it was much bigger than we expected, only part is excavated, rising waters have destroyed or are destroying much.

We did wonder if we have progressed very far in 4000 years as there seemed to be such modern looking constructions such as the great bath and the drainage channels. There were, in those days, no hooting vehicles or black plastic bags. Perhaps the people complained about the bullock carts.

We were equally impressed by the museum giving, as it does, a wonderful idea of the lives of the people.

We ate our lunch in the gardens.

We were then joined by a colleague of Simon's bringing transport as Simon had more work to do. This man, a Mr Kahn, had excellent English and was a great help in the museum. It made for a greater understanding with good translation.

I went to a small shop to buy some things for George and, as usual, tea was served as I sat and admired the merchandise. I was given a Sindi hat which later George wore with great aplomb.

The next night was spent at Larkana, the home of the Bhuto family. They didn't seem to be about and I expect their accommodation was better than mine, for I was not so lucky this time with the hotel. The window didn't fit and the bedhead was right up against it and there didn't seem anywhere else for it to go. I tried blocking the noise from the street below with the curtain but it wasn't satisfactory and the noises all continued late and started early, even before the calls to prayer.

Mr Kahn was determined next day that I should visit every possible ancient site, fort and tomb and when I was exhausted and covered in dust, invited me home to visit his wife and family. Simon said I must go although I pointed out that English ladies put on their best frocks when going out to tea. I didn't add that I also needed a 'wash and brush-up'.

"You do realize that these ladies have their own quarters," said Simon.

"Do your mean that they are in Purdah," I asked, suddenly apprehensive.

"You could call it that," he replied.

I had realized that Mr Kahn was a devout Muslim, his prayer times were strictly kept and I had also seen women about covered from head to foot with only a small mask across the eyes. To me it is a frightening garment, not so much for its concealment but for the feeling of female loss of freedom. I was worried about my reaction, it was real now and not just something I was viewing as an outsider.

Pakistan has a woman Prime-minister and I had also read Christine Cottam's excellent article in the 'Insight Guide' in which she says that "emancipated women, with a good education and training, can go a long way in Pakistan". This is fine so long as they do have a chance of a good education. Now I was about to meet some Pakistani women.

I was shown into the women's quarters and it was indicated to me to sit on the huge bed. As no-one spoke any English, such an exercise seemed to me to be somewhat futile and a moment of firm resolve came over me. I retreated, made for the door and said "No thank you, I shall join my son and the men," fully aware as I said it that no-one understood a word.

My intention they did understand, there was great consternation mixed with an Urdu palaver and much patting both of me and the bed, eventually Mr Kahn was called and it was all settled.

"Dr Son may join the ladies."

Simon gave me a look of 'there-I-knew-you'd-cope' and he was delighted at the event as it had never happened to him before. He sat quite happily on the bed, it was large enough for the whole party, tea was brought and presents exchanged. Wherever I went there was always tea, I am very partial to tea and it was no hardship to be offered an endless succession of cups but I am not so partial to slabs of yellow cake and often had difficulty, when it was pressed upon me, in secreting it away or hiding it about my person so as not to offend my hosts. This is not so easy if you are being minutely observed with every article of clothing and every gesture stored away for future discussion.

It was an occasion for all of us. A shawl was draped around me, Grandma was brought but viewed me with distrustful eyes. I suspect that I was considerably older than she and what right had I to be so active?

My gifts were of silk bought hastily on route when I realized that the invitation could not be refused.

Returning to the guest house was like coming home with my plants, animals and birds all expectant of my largesse. I had quite a routine by this time. It was not to last however, as Simon's work took him north and there was no point in my staying with him if I wasn't doing duty as part of his 'tribe'. Simon liked to shop and sightsee in his spare time.

"It's no fun on your own," he said.

The next flight was to Lahore and the hotel here was another of Simon's finds. We had old fashioned, round at the back, ground floor rooms and astonishment at the reception desk when we asked for two rooms.

"But this is your Mother?"

Simon admitted it.

"In Pakistan the family, Father, Mother, the children, Grandparents, they all share a room."

The room looked like it. More than enough space for all, two large beds behind a curtained off area and in the front or entrance part enough chairs and tables for a party, this included an opening out settee. A Pakistani family probably brought their own food and ate here too. The solitary candle, however, in its rickety candlestick boded ill for any hopes of evening entertainment for me such as reading or television. Later, yes, I needed it. It's just as well to be tired.

I hope I'll be forgiven if I don't mention all the tombs and forts we visited. There are two, there may be more, excellent guide books and all the information a tourist may need is in them. I must mention though that in many of the fine buildings we saw I was amazed by the mathematical beauty of some of the tiling and decorative work, wonderful colours and perfect symmetry in the patterns.

Now, in Lahore, I wanted to visit the Shalimar gardens, the name has a romantic ring to it of quiet longing and unrequited love. In my mind I think I hear the Indian Love Lyrics - something about "beside the Shalimar"? I know there was a lot of love and passion in it and people throwing themselves away for love. I can't see Tom thanking me for that, this undying passion lark is strictly for Orientals or, as far as Tom is concerned, for the engines of fast cars.

So I was expecting to renew these feelings of romance combined with tear bringing beauty.

There was nothing like that about the gardens.

We took an autorickshaw for the day, this is a very reasonable way of getting about and the driver likes to be part of your tour and join you for the day if possible. We went early and I was glad we did because later it became very crowded and the place was spoilt for me by the amount of litter which included dirty nappies and orange peel as well as picnic throw outs. The gardens had a beautiful formal layout too, with fountains and walks, the very opposite of my very English country garden. There must have been a great clearing up process at night as early in the day it was clean, big and empty.

Simon was very pensive next day and after breakfast and a little probing admitted to a certain amount of worry. Good worry, though, as all possible jobs are.

"There's a possibility of a longer contract - based at Islamabad, enough to make it worth while to bring out Jennie and the children. Would you mind if we went there to look at houses and schools?"

Would I mind? I did point out, however, that I would never choose a house for Jennie, she must do that for herself, but to look - oh - that's another matter.

So to Islamabad we went and Simon looking backwards up the accommodation list which has five stars at the top, found a small guest house on the outskirts of this very different, well planned clean town. For the time being he seemed to have given up the five star idea and this place proved to be very comfortable. Tea was immediately served even though prayers were being said in a corner of the room. Many hotels provide prayer mats for travellers who do not carry their own. I liked this idea, there was often a Koran too and, as I had never read this, took the opportunity of increasing my knowledge. The mat, however, I left in the cupboard.

We started off house-hunting next morning, looking for somewhere to live on a longer basis gives a feeling of belonging. Our house agent seemed to have every sign of being rich which was hopeful as he must have plenty of business. "He certainly behaves rich," agreed Simon, "But we have no idea how he made his money so we'd better be careful."

Beyond using his car instead of a taxi (autorickshaws are banned in Islamabad) we hardly needed his services and there were plenty of houses with reasonable rents. The Americans were at departure point so there would be more. We also visited two excellent schools, this time using a taxi, and, having satisfied ourselves on family living, started to enjoy the sights of the town.

We kept our same taxi man, first we had to see the Shah Faisal Mosque, I was much impressed, it has four rocket like minarets and is said to be the largest mosque in the world, there is a wonderful chandelier in the inside and a most unimpressive shop on the outside. Most of our own religious buildings do a nice little profitable sideline in goods, here there was only shoddy glittery rubbish.

We went into the town and bought food for a picnic which we ate in the Rose and Jasmine gardens. I was hoping that this domestic expedition wasn't in place of our visit to India, time might not now allow it.

"I may have to stay longer anyway," said Simon, "Shall you stay with me or go home?"

So that was it, my staying meant India, my going meant not. Sometimes it's as well to be silent.

Now he asked, "If we do go to India, are your papers in order?"

Mine were, his weren't.

We were in the right town to get his necessary documents as Islamabad is the Capital of Pakistan but I should mention that it is easier to obtain these in England.

The rest of the day was spent getting Simon's Indian Visa.

It is as well to know Islamabad or to have a good map as the taxi drivers are as likely to get lost as you are. We did manage to find the right building, parked on a lot of land with various tents and joined the vast queue of desperate looking men possibly trying to get out of the country. Or so I thought. Simon said they were probably going on holiday, camping out for the night or just chatting with their friends. I shall never know.

"We'd better hang on to the taxi," said Simon.

As I had every intention of sitting in it and not joining the ominous looking crowd, this was not difficult. The driver would be paid for his time and was quite happy, he seemed to have friends among the hordes where much business seemed to be taking place, as it was in Urdu I didn't understand a word but hoped for the best.

We had other offices to visit and from one Simon emerged rather red-faced and in a great hurry. He had met up with an American, had inadvertently given him wrong information, sent him off to the wrong building and was fervently hoping not to meet him again.

Simon's papers now being in order he had the bright idea of going to Peshawar where Ann and Patrick were now working. It was with Ann that I first travelled to Nigeria and she and Patrick were now old friends.

We went into town to book the flight. I stayed with the taxi, it had become quite like home, or at least a good temporary refuge.

Simon emerged triumphant. "There wasn't a flight on the short route, we'll have to go East and North. Its a long way round but you'll probably enjoy the view."

There's always a bright side.

It was raining next morning and fairly cold, our taxi man was nowhere to be seen. Being so far out of town was now a disadvantage, there was no taxi rank.

We were giving up hope when he arrived with a vehicle that looked as if it would not make it to the airport. Our apologetic little driver explained that his own vehicle had been impounded, fortunately for us another taxi approached but we had no time to hear the full story, which seemed to involve money, as we hastily grabbed the new arrival and made it to the airport just in time.

Simon's theory that I might enjoy the view was a vast understatement. It was fantastic. The small plane wound its way through the mountains. It was as well we had the usual prayers although these had lost their effectiveness for me when I realized it was a tape. It no longer seemed so reassuring.

We stopped at a very small airport. Here we were herded off the plane and everyone sat in rows in the waiting room. I had no intention of joining them and after visiting the loo (very clean but the footstep variety I don't much like) I returned to the tarmac to breathe in the surrounding beauty. The armed guards took no notice of me, I thought it unlikely that anyone would actually shoot me. Eventually we were all shepherded back to the plane.

As the plane slid between the hills Simon leaned over me, "I tell you what, I wouldn't mind walking in these hills."

He can be sure of one thing. Mother won't be coming. However I began to understand the almost obsessional hold such places have on people and why they return again and again.

We were now in the North West Frontier Province, the NWFP, Peshawar seemed a very different town from Islamabad.

We took an autorickshaw to Ann and Patrick's, as it was Friday they were both at home.

The people of Peshawar looked different too, they looked more rugged, men were wearing guns and had a tough look of the hills, a shoot-first-and-ask-after look. I liked the hats they wore, a flat cloth cap, and I decided to buy some for my friends back home. Most suitable for our cold windy winters.

The Afghan border was closed but from my bedroom window I could see the Khyber Pass. What more could a travelling lady want?

Just occasionally I hit a jackpot.

"I could settle in here nicely," I said, "For a good long time," I added hopefully.

"Why don't you stay?" asked Ann, "We can shop and I can show you around".

It was not to be, of course. A phone call back to base informed Simon that a V.I.P. was arriving to view the project's work so, after a very hurried visit to the fantastic and famous market (the Queen has shopped here), an excellent night's sleep and a very civilized breakfast, we were off again and returned to base.

CHAPTER 14

I was anxious this time not to get too settled, my room was beginning to take on a cluttered look of me. It's too easy to sink into a routine, there was still so much to see.

The trouble with a mixed type of project is that there is a certain amount of internal strife and gossip and Simon was anxious not to get mixed up in it. He was fortunately his own master. Rumour had apparently been flourishing about his mother. It was said that while he came back looking tired Mother's health seemed to be daily improving.

"They want to meet you," said Simon. Betty is going to ring you.

I thought she was hopeful and this unlikely as the phone hadn't been working for some time, she visited me, her husband dropping her off on his way to work. It seemed to me that the lives of the western women were almost as restricted as those of the Pakistani women. They relied on a project car and didn't find it pleasant to go out on their own. To our eyes the men's behaviour is very ill-mannered and I now understood poor Elizabeth's feelings. At 13 I suppose she is of marriageable age but she hated being stared at, patted and called 'Baby'. I suppose these men see popular silly films and think all western women are 'available' and like this sort of behaviour. Having myself only been out with Simon and being too old to be of interest, I hadn't encountered this, except the staring, until I now made friends with a young attractive woman.

"How do you cope?" I asked her.

"I try to take no notice," she answered, "As I speak Urdu I sometimes turn on them and give them a mouthful. If it does nothing else it surprises them."

Perhaps Elizabeth should learn Urdu.

I didn't think life here compared well with life in Zambia, there we all seemed so united and to have so much to do, partly I think because most families had young children and school activities were a focal point for everyone.

I couldn't see Jennie in this sort of life.

"What if Jennie and the children come out?" I asked Simon.

He laughed, "What do you think?" he said, "They'll cope."

I went to a coffee morning and was surprised to find that in my few weeks I had been around and seen more sights than most of the wives had in a year.

"Did you ask her?" I heard someone whisper in an aside.

"No," was the answer, "I reckon with all she does she wouldn't have time."

The Question.

"Do you play bridge?"

Betty, who answered the question was right. In between teaching, gardening, travelling and trying write a book I didn't seem to have much time. I hope I wasn't a disappointment to them but I think I was.

I think I was a disappointment too to the silk merchants we had visited while away further north. How I loved these materials spread out before me as I sat, drank tea and admired the ever increasing display. My choice must have seemed dull and unenterprising to someone who has not had to wade through our mud on a winter's day. Our lifestyle is not suited to the glittering shining silks I was shown, they don't go with wind, cold and welly boots.

I was a disappointment also to "Quickladiestaylor" just five minutes away down the road. My drab materials and styles compared unfavourably with the gaudy ladies wear hanging on the walls.

As I prepared to leave the guest house the bearer hastily took off his apron. Almost disbelieving I realized I was to be accompanied and not to be let out on my own.

"Quickladiestaylor" had about ten workers neatly tucked behind their old 'Singer' sewing machines in a room about the size of my kitchen. They were all men, there was plenty of fresh air as the double doors opened to the road. I should have liked to enquire as to the sanitary arrangements of some of these establishments but I didn't like to and perhaps as well for my peace of mind not to enquire too deeply. The river was near and crops appeared to be flourishing.

Simon had a day off and we went to Hala. The furniture was as I had remembered it in Sukkar, I had to stick closely to Simon whose ideas expand with the size of the goods on offer, forgetting that he only has an old stone cottage back home and he loves large happy furniture. Whilst turning my back to admire some wall hangings I found we had acquired quite a few things including a large standard lamp which fortunately came to pieces for packing and an equally large blue vase that didn't. I wondered where I could secrete it back at the guest house, under the bed perhaps, and conveniently forget it in the packing chaos in order to avoid having it on my lap during the flight home.

The car was still where we parked it and all its wheels. Something to be said for Islam, in Africa not only the wheels would be missing, everything movable would be gone and no-one would have seen a thing.

There was more going on at the guest house now; there were other visitors, one had just returned from India full of its delights.

I reminded Simon.

"When's the flight?" I asked him.

"Which flight?" he also asked in a casual something-up-my-sleeve-you-may-not-like way.

"Aren't we flying to Delhi?" I am surprised and cautious at his manner.

"We're flying to Lahore, then we can walk across the border. This way we get to Amritsa and see the Golden Temple." A slight sinking feeling assailed me. This is not the first time I'd traipsed across borders on the strength, not of my legs, but of Simon's optimism.

"Are you sure?" I ask tentatively. "Wouldn't it be easier to fly?"

"To fly?" he replied almost in capital letters and in a voice conveying but not spoken 'you're not the woman you were!'

"I'm sure the border is closed," I ventured, having at one time heard of troubles there.

"We'll soon find out," he replied cheerfully, adding "Of course, you can go the other way if you want to".

I like the "of course". Of course he knows I'll go his way.

"There'll be plenty of taxis so it won't be far to walk".

Haven't I heard that one before? I should be wary by now of such statements as 'It's just round the corner' or 'the walk will do you good'.

The way to enter India is by way of the Great Indian Gate. It is very impressive as I discovered later when we visited it and I was able to visualize the entrance of some Emperor or other great notable.

The other way is to fly in, this is far less romantic as most airports are indistinguishable from one another. But these ways are not for me.

We left the Lahore hotel very early in the morning and took a taxi to the border, we arrived much too early for, as Simon sensibly pointed out, we had a great deal to do and the earlier the better. This over enthusiasm proved to be wasted as there was no-one in the administrative building and we could not make it over the border without all the formalities of stamped passports and signing various documents. We sat in the taxi and I read the paper while money exchangers pestered Simon. Eventually word got round and an official could be seen making his way towards us buttoning up his jacket. The taxi man, glad perhaps to get away from the danger zone, dumped our luggage on a hopeful porter and drove off.

I am committed.

We left Pakistan and started off across the no-man's-land that divides the two countries. Porters go as far as the edge, others await you. It is all very clean and tidy. I enjoy this brief spell in a traffic free, empty stretch of borderland. Then we were in India.

It is surprising that in so short a trek how different everything looks. I had thought that partition was only religious but the people looked burlier and the dress tidier, the turban is an attractive headgear.

In spite of the officialdom it seemed very welcoming, we were the only travellers this way but perhaps sometimes large buses are unloaded and reloaded for there are facilities for organizing and regulating much larger numbers.

My passport was now beginning to improve, it looked shabbier and had more stamps. At least ten people have looked at it.

I have a feeling that I'm going to like India, for one thing I am looked in the eye and treated as a person, not an attachment of Simon's.

There really are taxis here as Simon promised but they are shabby compared with the yellow cabs of Pakistan. They are fashioned on the model of an older British car and look homely. There was a great deal of commotion as we crossed the line.

"Taxi!" "Taxi!" "This way Sir!"

"Mine is over here Sir," and to me "Would you like tea, coke, food ..."

"Yes, I'd love tea," I say to Simon.

"Not here, it isn't far to Amritsa. Taxi first, we'll have it when we get there."

We chose the least shabby of the Taxis and drove to Amritsa.

At the nearest hotel Simon said, "Now we can have tea and leave our luggage here while we visit the Temple, or we might stay here. It all depends."

"On what?" I asked.

"On whether we can or can't get out of here tonight. You can wait here and have some breakfast." He looked hopefully at his watch. "I'll walk round to the airline offices and see if we can get on a flight to Delhi this evening. If we can't I'll see about a train."

I love trains but I've seen pictures of Indian trains and was doubtful.

"I hope it isn't one of those that people cling to and travel on the roof." This with my usual caution.

"There'll be first class accommodation and plenty of tea," he reassured me.

It was not to be, he returned with a chancy plane booking and a rickshaw driver.

"I've kept my rickshaw driver," he said looking longingly at the remains of my breakfast.

"What driver?" I queried, "I thought you said you were walking."

"He was outside the airline offices, I thought I'd bring him for you as his English is so good."

It was. Perhaps he found us rather than us finding him, he was a history graduate, a kind, helpful man whose name we never knew. I sometimes think that I shall return to find out.

When we arrived at the Golden Temple in his very shabby vehicle it was obvious that he meant to accompany us and be our guide. Now I like to wander about these places on my own and not be led around with a lot of touristy chat, so I was a little put out. How wrong I was. I accepted his presence because his English was so good but soon we accepted him as a friend as well and, but for him we should never have seen the complete picture. For this is not a place apart from everyday living, this practical side is part of it holiness. I loved it. All are fed here with volunteers preparing and serving free meals for thousands every day. There are two sittings and no-one goes away hungry. Without our guide, who showed us the kitchens with the preparation of food where a huge bearded Sikh cook stood over an enormous cauldron, the place where the donated food is left, and the necessary but unexciting washing up, I doubt if we should have appreciated the work that goes on here. He also showed us all the holy places and such crafts as the gold beating.

I cannot understand or in any way explain my feeling of well-being as we strolled around this amazing place. Perhaps it was the walk that had done me good or perhaps it was the sunshine or even the tea but from then on I had no tummy troubles and no leg pains.

I found I was appallingly ignorant of the Temple's recent history and its association with the assassination of Mrs. Gandhi. I was surprised to see signs of battle in such a place but I began to understand what had happened with the help of our guide and later read up the details.

Now I learned that Pilgrims could be accommodated here and, beginning to feel like a pilgrim myself, suggested to Simon that we stayed here. This, too, was free (a donation is not refused) and Simon looked tempted.

"We'll come back if we can't get on the plane," he promised.

We collected our luggage and our guide took us to the airport where we said 'Goodbye' to him.

The airport was dreary, I think I'd have preferred the train, but after a long wait we were told that there were available seats.

The pleasures of the day were somewhat spoiled here, I was used to searches conducted by inquisitive and usually pretty Pakistani girls but here was a wardress of an old fashioned type with hair scraped back and a grim expression, the sort that makes you feel guilty before you even start to turn out your pockets. I felt she was out of place here and would have been happier in a concentration camp. I was, however, determined to get a smile out of her. During the first search my attempts to do this brought no response but, but the third time and in what looked like a hastily erected latrine tent put up on the tarmac just before boarding, I was driven to exclaim in a voice usually reserved for a recalcitrant member of the lower fourth, "Not YOU again!" and to my surprise there was a relaxation of those face muscles. I'd won! She was, I suppose, only doing her duty but this was an internal flight and what were we supposed to have been carrying? Perhaps we could have come over the border (it was near) loaded with drugs but everything was carefully checked there. I saw Simon, resignedly facing an equally grim-faced set of men, his main worry being Mother. I could see him thinking, "This isn't five star treatment, would it have been better to go by train." I was careful not to give a thumbs up sign in case is was interpreted as success in whatever nefarious enterprise we might have been engaged in. Strangely we managed to keep our batteries this time though most other travellers lost theirs.

I was elated by my success in the smile exercise and as we boarded I felt sure that, given time, the wardress and I might have made friends.

After this experience I was pleasurably surprised to find myself sitting next to a saffron robed monk, I wondered where he was going and unjustifiably felt he should be walking and our present mode of travel out of keeping with his habit. How I should have loved a little chat but he looked very pointedly out of his window on the other side. Perhaps he didn't like women. During the flight he was offered many things by the stewardess via me, some of which he accepted. I thought he was beginning to feel reassured by the end of the flight when we had the worst landing I have ever known and he threw himself, or was thrown, almost into my arms. I patted his hand comfortingly and we were now friends and didn't need the little chat.

Simon and I had arrived in Delhi.

We boarded the bus and drove into town. Simon had his Indian Guide Book with him and I could see this five star Mother syndrome flourishing again. We went to the most expensive hotel.

"I promised you five star and here it is," he said triumphantly.

We were a bit scruffy and although in Africa this is acceptable, even being taken as a sign that you have been on Safari, here it was not so. The hotel was 'full up'. We doubted it although, I must admit, there were large homogeneous groups with ditto expensive luggage being herded about. Except for the loos, quite the best I'd met, so far, in Asia. I was unimpressed by the opulence which to me is touristy and un-Indian and I was glad when Simon, consulting his guide book once more, and with, I thought, considerably more buoyancy in his step, found a small no-nonsense, unpretentious, clean and delightful hotel where we settled down to enjoy Delhi.

We spent next day finding out more about the elephant and tiger Safari and Simon slightly guilty and with his ideal rose covered Mother still in mind started looking at the more glamorous establishments. At one travel agent he found a place that promised the earth, the pictures looked good but I was suspicious by the way it was being plugged. How wonderful it sounded, elephants were pictured outside the front, there was a swimming pool, beautiful grounds and chalets, it sounded wonderful.

"How long shall I book for?" asked Simon delighted that, at last, he was offering me all that he thought I wanted.

"Just the one night," I replied, unable to explain that feeling of doubt and wondering why they wanted all the money in advance, "We can stay on if we like it or find something else when we get there."

Simon reluctantly agreed.

The driving in India is just as Kamikaze as in Pakistan and the fumes too are similar so I was not keen on being driven round and round Delhi. We had now acquired a new Autorickshaw driver, one with very definite ideas of what we had to see and do, although this is not quite my 'scene' especially when I find myself taken to the sort of places where I feel the driver has his rake-off. I allowed myself to relax and be shown the places tourists have to see. This was until we passed the Railway Museum. I'd been done out of my train trip and I love trains.

"Is it open?" I asked the driver.

"Yes," he replied as he whizzed past.

"Good, we'll go there."

"No, no, still more buildings to see."

He drove on.

Determined not to be bullied by a rickshaw driver, I said, "No, no to more buildings, turn back to the Railway Museum." He looked stubborn so Simon joined in on my behalf. It was probably this masculine intervention that made the driver realize that I was serious.

A smile came over his face as he turned and drove to the entrance.

"I shall go and see my Mother."

"Does she live near?" I asked.

"Just around the corner."

Maybe that's why he gave way, there is always a handy relative.

I loved the museum, full as it is of lovely old engines and carriages.

This driver had another relative and, when we enquired if he knew of anyone who would take us to the Wildlife Park, he sent along a nephew with a useful vehicle.

This young man, Sanjay, was just starting up his own touring business, we liked him and his little bus looked reliable. We booked him for the following day.

It was a fairly long drive that took us most of the day. I enjoyed it. I enjoyed the contrast between the town we had left and the country side, there were animals, piles of dung, overloaded buses and different modes of dress. Beyond the main roads and modern cities in India, as well as Pakistan, there are glimpses of unchanged countryside and living conditions. To drive through this is merely scratching the surface of understanding the real India and its magic. how can one possibly see all the diversity in a few hours drive or in a few days stay? One thing is certain, no-one can 'do' India in one week nor write it up in one chapter. Neither can I personally think up adequate words to describe the whole. What makes up this whole? To me, it's the extraordinary and wonderful variety, the rush and bustle of the towns, the mixture there, strange to us, of animals and motorized vehicles, the architecture, the countryside, the vivid colourfulness of life everywhere. It has to be seen. I know I must go again.

I think if visitors have paid fantastic amounts of money for a tour they do not wish to see unwelcome sights such as what I can only describe as a 'vulture park'. Carcasses are soon stripped clean in these places, I am sure it is very hygienic. Vultures are not attractive birds at the best of times, but they are all part of the scene.

We started early, stopping when we needed tea, other

refreshment or time for natural functions. Sanjay we found was another graduate, this time in economics. He was equally enthusiastic about this trip, although we had understood from his uncle (however far removed) that he was very experienced, in what we did not know. We now discovered that he had never journeyed far from Delhi. We thought his prices very low but he wanted the trip as much as the job, after this he was the Wildlife Park Expert and secretly he was longing to see tiger and ride on an elephant. This was to be included in his fee along with his food and accommodation. He drove carefully, too carefully Simon thought, but it was ideal for me as I could relax and enjoy all the sights along the way.

We found our way to the hotel, it looked exactly like its picture but where were the elephants?

"We don't keep them here," we were told.

"Where are they then," I asked.

"In the Park."

"But that is twenty miles away," said Simon in annoyance. This grew when we started to view the unfinished establishment. The swimming pool was part of the river but, as crocodiles were mentioned as possible wildlife, not to be recommended. It was no danger to us however as it was several hundred feet down a cliff and needed climbing ropes and crampons to reach it. We peered over the cliff and saw several well fed looking crocs in the river, Simon suggested that that may be the reason for so few guests.

We were shown to our chalets and these were big, adjoining and very, very cold. There was no hot water and limited electricity.

We enjoyed supper, we were asked what we wanted, there was a very limited choice but when it came it was good and hot.

There was only one other guest, a young man from Germany who had booked in advance in his own country, he like us had had to pay in advance. We left him early next morning pondering on his immediate future. We were sure about ours, we would take our chance in the park and, if the worst came to the worst, sleep in the van. He admired our independent travelling methods or haphazard as I have often called them, we offered to take him with us but he'd paid the earth for accommodation and food and didn't want to lose out on the deal.

Sanjay had not been treated well, we had paid for him also and had been told that he was being well treated. We found him next morning in the van wrapped in a blanket cold and unhappy. We packed up and drove back to the town for breakfast. We found a nice sleazy little cafe, stocked up with fruit from a stall, and found the right place to book for the park.

We drove to the gates, presented our permit and entered the park. We were there at last.

The warden was not positive about beds but we were not worried, there was dormitory accommodation and Sanjay's van as a last resort.

"I'm not worried for myself," said Simon, "It's Mother."

I tried to look sufficiently weary and Mother like.

"I will give Mother my own room if there is nothing else," replied the Warden gallantly. A lovely thought, I just hoped he wouldn't still be in it.

The reason for this uncertainty was that earlier bookings than ours might bring other travellers and we had to wait until dusk for the final allocation of rooms. There was also a large party of birdwatchers, I've heard them called 'twitchers', these would be leaving next day. When their leader called his flock was expected to come running, perhaps to tick off on a list another unobtrusive small brown bird, maybe only a speck in the far woodland.

Now came the elephants, I'd like a bed but this is what I'd come for, compared with this sleeping arrangements were of secondary importance.

As we prepared to mount we had another example of the dedication of the twitchers. A bird watcher joined our group, making the four on 'Blossom'. The group consisted of Simon, a young man called Brian and myself. The twitchers' leader called out in great indignation, "We can't have one of our group with . . ." He didn't finish the sentence as the poor twitcher with us slunk back to the fold. With whom? we asked ourselves, how would he have described us? "That motley crew" perhaps. Out to look at tigers. Whatever next?

Sanjay now happily joined us, he was being held back as residents had a cheaper rate and the higher paying riders were mounted first.

We were off.

What wonderful feet elephants have. Viewed from above each ponderous footstep was a delight to me. Sanjay's presence was a Godsend. He talked to the Mahout and translated throughout the trip.

Alas we saw no tiger, only an enormous pussyfoot print. What matter? I saw them peering at me through every leafy branch as we threaded our way through the trees and undergrowth. At one point the Mahout pointed out a great brown pile.

"I didn't come all this way to see Tiger turds," grumbled Simon.

"Quite fresh," translated Sanjay.

I was sure I could see the culprit just behind a bush. We could hear the wild elephants trumpeting but we were not able to go too near as one was believed to be in season and it might be dangerous. I thought Blossom was about my age and surely past it but perhaps it's different for elephants?

This was the best way to see wildlife and the complete environment. I think I felt part of it, but very sad that man, in thinking himself top dog, is ruining so much.

We returned to the camp just before dusk: there was still tomorrow, meanwhile what of the night? Before visiting the warden again I had a quick look at the dormitory accommodation. If I had to, well, I had to but was not travelling with a sleeping bag, after all if it is to be 'five star all the way' the necessity doesn't arise. I now wondered at my foolhardiness.

The warden was in his office, he grinned cheerfully and handed over a key, he also instructed a man to bring a heater (extra) and to see if there was anything else I needed. I was in.

The room was more like a small flat with two large beds, chairs and all mod cons. Simon viewed the extra bed and all thoughts of dormitories vanished.

"Pity to waste it," he said as he dumped his belongings on it.

The room was right over the restaurant and our student friends were glad to make use of our facilities.

"Thank goodness for Mother," one of them muttered as she rushed to get her towel and clean clothes from her dormitory. "It's a bit basic there," she said.

We had a grand and friendly meal.

How I should have liked to stay until the monsoon.

"What happens when all these tracks are impassable?" I had asked, "Surely no vehicle can get by?"

"Vehicle?" was the reply, "No vehicle, plenty of elephants."

I really fancied calling, "I need to go shopping, is the elephant ready?"

But the time came to leave. We hadn't seen tiger but we'd had a wonderful time and we still had the Taj Mahal to 'do'.

On the road back to Delhi I noticed a sign which read 'Overtakers provide jobs for undertakers'. I think I'll write this caution for the back of my mini for I feel prayers are not enough for the type of driver who will overtake on blind corners.

We found another hotel in Connaught Place in Delhi; there is an excellent restaurant which must be renowned world-wide for it was crowded with so many varied peoples. Even a young man travelling with his Mother didn't seem an oddity.

We sat at a table and were joined by a young German man who didn't like our presence.

"I've sat at this table for ten years," he complained as he glowered and blew smoke over us.

"Time you moved," muttered Simon, but I was gathering up my things, I preferred a non-smoker otherwise I should have been prepared to stay and glower back.

Simon joined me, still grumbling.

"Ten years, I ask you ... ?"

There was a fixed price eat-as-much-as-you-like salad bar. The couple next to our table took a plate each, piled it up high several times over and stuffed and stuffed with blank faces, no smiles, no words, just eating as if they hadn't seen food for weeks. Perhaps they hadn't.

My room had a passage from the bathroom lined with mirrors, firm ideas about dieting came to me as I returned to the bedroom. No-one could overeat with such a reminder.

Sanjay was waiting for us early next morning for the trip to Agar and the Taj Mahal.

I suppose one had to go there, it looks exactly like its pictures especially when viewed head on with the water down the middle, the fountains were not playing. There were crowds of people.

All right, it's a masterpiece, a vast expanse of white marble tomb. I admit its magnificence, only I'm not really 'into' white marble tombs. I love buildings which have a lived in look, especially those extraordinary hotch-potch-down-the-alley ones with bits and pieces added on, the sort that would be hastily condemned and pulled down in this country.

The setting of the Taj Mahal, however, with all the beautiful trees and the lovely warm sandstone of the surrounding buildings was a wonderful contrast and so on the whole I was not disappointed but Simon was at my reaction.

"But everyone, just about everyone, admits that it's the most beautiful building in the world. Why, oh why, do you have to be different?"

I was sorry and a bit humble when I explained that the highlight of my trip was the elephant in the jungle and I suppose I was just being awkward.

I was sorry to see that even the Taj Mahal was showing the effects of pollution. Sorry but not surprised.

Wandering around the sides in places where few other visitors wander, we came across some workmen, Sanjay being with us understanding presented no problem. They had removed badly effected pieces of the building and were going to replace them with newly quarried stone. I was given a small piece of the old marble and sandstone. I suspect this pollution will get worse and here, as elsewhere, nothing serious will be done about the cause, only patching up.

I was amused to hear the sound of a 1930's lawn mower and to see a man pushing it. I had always understood that this was done by fine oxen. I looked around but saw none.

Simon had quite forgiven me by the time we came to leave.

"Is there anything you want," he asked as we came to the shops at the gate. Thee shops were full of Taj Mahal merchandise.

"I must have a model for Tom," I answered.

There were models of all sizes and materials, there were Taj Mahal shirts, scarfs, handkerchiefs and possibly socks if one looked hard enough. It is difficult to get away from traders and I only wanted a small plastic model but my feeble joke was not so funny when I viewed the vast selection. I chose a small one in a box, I couldn't find one in the shape of a teapot and Tom just might have preferred socks.

Our return to Delhi was now a Goodbye visit. Goodbye to our haunts, our friends and saddest of all, Goodbye to Sanjay.

"We'll come again," we told him.

"Perhaps bring all the family?" I suggested to Simon.

"Why not?" he said.

This time we flew to Karachi. Simon has this its-only-fair theory of always taking the first taxi in the rank. Not always easy in the chaos and jumble outside the airport. I prefer a driver who can speak English. This isn't easy either because a reply of 'Yes' does not mean fluency in the language.

This fair idea of Simon's led us into the sleaziest backwaters I have ever encountered.

The driver pulled up and, unable to make us understand, departed. I should certainly have panicked had I been a first timer and on my own. As it was our worst fear was whether to close the windows and stifle or open them and be bitten by the hoards of mosquitos. We closed them and sat back to await events, nobody took any notice of us so it didn't look as if we were going to be held to ransom. This cheered me as I didn't fancy being chained to a wall for any length of time. I haven't Terry Waite's strength of character.

"I wouldn't be surprised if he hasn't gone to say his prayers," said Simon cheerfully. he began to have ideas of cooling drinks and water so that when a completely new driver turned up we had chosen a hotel near the beach with a swimming pool. It probably had been prayer time, we never knew.

"I've never been on a camel," I said sadly as we waited for some of these magnificent beasts to pass by.

"Turn round and drive to the beach," Simon told our driver.

I had never really liked camels until I came to Pakistan, the scruffy animals I'd seen before didn't compare with these.

I had to admit that the ones before me on a touristy beach where Simon proposed I should satisfy my whim were not up to the standard of my vision. My vision, that is of a lonely desert trek, but I mustn't grumble, we mounted one and it trotted off so I know how it feels. Perhaps two hundred yards is far enough.

We flew back to base and it fell to me to organize the packing as Simon still had to finish his project and there was a good deal of office work.

I managed to hide the blue vase, there was so much more after Simon's little shopping jaunts that I hoped he wouldn't notice or perhaps he turned a deliberate blind eye. He never mentioned its loss, it must be still there if anyone feels like retrieving it.

I am home again and my sitting room is even more cluttered though Africa has not entirely given way to Asia; throw-overs now cover my shabby furniture, carvings and pictures are everywhere. I feel that if I travel any more I shall have to enlarge this room or I could open a small museum.

I am thinking along these lines when the phone rings.

"I got that contract," says Simon.

"We're all off next month. Shall you come for Christmas?"

I immediately forget all the things I ought to be doing.

"I'll start packing," I reply.

"Why don't you come first class?" he asks, "It'll be five star all the way."